P9-CMT-363

Four Paws from Heaven

M.R. WELLS   KRIS YOUNG
CONNIE FLEISHAUER

HARVEST HOUSE PUBLISHERS

EUGENE, OREGON

Unless otherwise indicated, all Scripture quotations are taken from the HOLY BIBLE, NEW INTERNATIONAL VERSION®. NIV®. Copyright © 1973, 1978, 1984 by the International Bible Society. Used by permission of Zondervan. All rights reserved.

Verses marked NKJV are taken from the New King James Version. Copyright © 1982 by Thomas Nelson, Inc. Used by permission. All rights reserved.

Verses marked KJV are taken from the King James Version of the Bible.

Verses marked NRSV are from the New Revised Standard Version of the Bible, copyright © 1989 by the Division of Christian Education of the National Council of the Churches of Christ in the USA. Used by permission. All rights reserved.

Verses marked NLT are taken from the *Holy Bible,* New Living Translation, copyright © 1996. Used by permission of Tyndale House Publishers, Inc., Wheaton, IL 60189 USA. All rights reserved.

Cover by Left Coast Design, Portland, Oregon

Published in association with the literary agency of Mark Sweeney & Associates, 28540 Altessa Way, Suite 201, Bonita Springs, FL 34135.

Cover photo © Alley Cat Productions/Brand X Pictures/Getty Images

The information shared by the authors is from their personal experience and should not be considered professional advice. Readers should consult their own dog care professionals regarding issues related to the health, safety, grooming, and training of their pets.

FOUR PAWS FROM HEAVEN
Copyright © 2006 by M.R. Wells, Kris Young, and Connie Fleishauer
Published by Harvest House Publishers
Eugene, Oregon 97402
www.harvesthousepublishers.com

Library of Congress Cataloging-in-Publication Data
Wells, M. R. (Marion R.), 1948-
    Four paws from heaven / M.R. Wells, Kris Young, and Connie Fleishauer.
          p. cm.
    Includes bibliographical references.
    ISBN-13: 978-0-7369-1640-0 (pbk.)
    ISBN-10: 0-7369-1640-7 (pbk.)
    1. Dog owners—Prayer-books and devotions—English. I. Young, Kris, 1953–
II. Fleishauer, Connie. III. Title.
BV4596.A54W45 2006
242—dc22   2005028905

All rights reserved. No part of this publication may be reproduced, stored in a retrieval system, or transmitted in any form or by any means—electronic, mechanical, digital, photo-copy, recording, or any other—except for brief quotations in printed reviews, without the prior permission of the publisher.

Printed in the United States of America

06 07 08 09 10 11 12 13 14 / VP-CF / 10 9 8 7 6 5

We dedicate this book to our faithful canine coauthors; our wise and loving heavenly Master; and our wonderful families and friends, who jogged our memories, cheered us on, and prayed us through.

Acknowledgments

Many hands made *Four Paws from Heaven* a reality. We are grateful to our agents, Mark and Janet Sweeney; our editor, Kim Moore; and the entire Harvest House publishing team for helping our dream come true. We're indebted to Pastor Jerry Wilke; Paige Evans, DVM; Dottie Adams; and Jonathan Klein for their invaluable comments and suggestions. We so appreciate the prayers and support of our families and friends.

Most of all, we thank and praise God—to Him be the glory!

Contents

Part 1
Heart to Heart

Part II
Obedience Training

Part V
Master Knows Best

Foreword

In the Old Testament book of Numbers we find the account of a prophet named Balaam, who was summoned by a pagan king to curse the children of Israel. God gave Balaam leave to go to the king, but warned him to do only what He (God) commanded.

So the next morning Balaam set out. But the angel of the Lord blocked his way—not just once, but three times. And though Balaam didn't see the angel of the Lord, his donkey did. The donkey balked. Balaam beat the donkey. At last God opened the animal's mouth, and his faithful and long-suffering pet actually spoke to Balaam (Numbers 22:5-35).

Those of you who think this was a unique occurrence probably aren't dog owners.

Okay, so man's best friends aren't apt to launch into human speech at the blink of a Bible verse. But we believe God uses them nonetheless...in the way Romans 1 describes: "For since the creation of the world God's invisible qualities—his eternal power and divine nature—have been clearly seen, being understood from what has been made, so that men are without excuse" (Romans 1:20).

Parables of sheep, soil, and fig trees connected powerfully with the herders and farmers of Jesus' day. Today, dogs play a vital role in many of our lives. They're often treated as part of the family. People connect powerfully with tales about these treasured pets. Even if God hasn't opened their mouths, we believe He can use them to speak to our hearts and build a bridge to deeper spiritual insights.

Back in Genesis, God gave man dominion over all other living creatures as a special gift and trust (Genesis 1:28). We who write this book count our dogs a gift and trust from Him. God has used them to love us, brighten our lives, and help us know Him better. In the hope that their stories might bless you too, or at least make you smile, we share the vignettes that follow. It's okay. They "said" you could read them.

Enjoy!

Meet the Pups

Biscuit Wells

A fluffy white American Eskimo "mini," Biscuit mixes cover-dog looks with a Miss Congeniality temperament. A friend dubbed her "Party Dog," and it fits. She loves to play hostess or entertain guests with her small repertoire of tricks. She even made one up herself. When told to roll, she spins in a circle and flips herself over. Biscuit also tries to play "Mama Dog" by helping me discipline my cats. And she's quick to flip into watchdog mode and woof if she hears a sound that concerns her. But mostly she just hangs with me. When Biscuit was a pup and I went to visit her litter of four, it was she who took to me the most. She has been my friend and writing buddy ever since.

Morgan Wells

Part sheltie, part "potluck," and all personality, Morgan is a shy guy with a heart of gold. His black-and-tan fur is of varying lengths, and his feet are tipped with little white tufts. He loves to snuggle and could live on my lap. When he's happy he leaps straight into the air or rubs his paw against his ear. He runs like the wind, but he will tuck his tail and drag his doggie heels to stall. Agile as a cat, he can leap a baby gate or spring onto a garden wall. The way he sneaks where he doesn't belong has earned him the nickname "Slink." I took him in as a two-year-old rescue, and he lets me know daily how grateful he is—which reminds me I must thank my Savior too.

Gracie Young

Chunky and low-slung like a Eureka canister vacuum cleaner with legs, Gracie was probably the love child of a corgi-shepherd tryst. After a Good Samaritan found her wandering in a parking lot, Gracie made her way into my home and heart through prayer and providence. Sweet-natured and a little goofy, she had an uncanny ability to read my mind. I'll always think of this little tan dog as one of my best pals. Gracie truly was a gift from God.

McPherson Fleishauer

Full of love and spunk, McPherson was a beautiful shepherd mix—the child of a Fleishauer dog and a wanderer. He was born on my husband Steve's parents' farm. He was our first pup as a young married couple, and we all learned a lot together. Despite a few missteps on our part, he matured into a fine working farm dog. When we had our own children, McPherson was right there to help, serving as a canine nanny to all three. Even in old age, he never relinquished his role as our family's friend and protector.

Max Fleishauer

Small in stature but large in faithfulness, Max was a Boston terrier who often behaved like a tiny, proud lion. He never let his size deter him from his mission to guard us. He didn't like to sit on laps, but if he thought someone needed him, he stretched out near them and wouldn't leave their side. He was black-and-white, with a short, wide muzzle and large, round eyes set far apart. Some thought he was ugly, but we didn't agree. Our daughter Christy spied him at a pet store where he'd been returned because of a birth defect. We thought he was perfect for us...and we never changed our minds.

Huxley Fleishauer

Huxley came to us by accident...sort of. I had gone to the SPCA (Society for the Prevention of Cruelty to Animals) just to visit, not intending to walk off with another dog. Then this sweet little puppy looked at me. I told him, "Forget it. You're not coming home with me under any circumstances." But his eyes convinced my heart, and he was ours. We were never entirely sure of his breeding, except that he was a mix, but he looked a lot like an American foxhound. He was tall and lean with a short tan-and-white coat. Huxley ruled as king in our backyard, chasing cats and climbing an occasional tree, and he was Steve's right-hand dog for catching gophers. He also made a great security system with his repertoire of barks—and he was a great companion to us all.

Stuart Fleishauer

Welsh corgis are the Queen of England's choice of dog. I certainly understand that. We found Stuart online. When we saw his picture, we knew he was meant for us. Stuart has a beautiful coat of red, tan, and white with black shadows. He's strong and active and sturdily built, with short little legs that hide beneath him when he stretches out on the floor. He loves to play fetch, and he knows the names  of every one of his toys. He loves to chase cats or run free in the yard. But most of all he just loves being with us—wiggling and cuddling and licking our ears or warming our hearts with his bright eyes and sweet smile. And when I write he is there beside me, as if to encourage me—like the great friend he is.

Part I

Heart to Heart

A Dog in the Hand
God Holds Us Fast

If I rise on the wings of the dawn,
if I settle on the far side of the sea,
even there your hand will guide me,
your right hand will hold me fast.

PSALM 139:9-10

Shortly after I adopted Morgan, he became deathly sick. His next days were spent in "doggie ICU." Thankfully, he healed. Thrilled to have him back, I brought him home and let him out to do his business.

The next thing I knew, he'd gone AWOL.

I live in a hilly area. My south-side neighbor's yard is lower than mine. Wire fencing separates our properties. Morgan found a gap in that fence and slipped through, doubtless lured by some bird or squirrel. He was having a ball!

I was having a fit!

Who knew if the next yard was gated? What if Morgan got out of that one too? He hadn't had time to learn the neighborhood. Suppose he took off? Would he vanish forever? Never mind my investment in vet bills—I had lost my heart to this dog. I feared in the time it took to run through my house and around to my neighbor's home, my little guy might be gone. Heart in mouth, I squeezed through the same gap in the fence and jumped down after him.

Somehow, I landed without breaking a limb and gathered the little runaway into my arms. Sighing with relief, I carried him out to the street. Only then did I realize I had locked myself out.

Though my back door was open, my front door wasn't. The gate to my yard was locked too. I couldn't hoist Morgan over the top of the gate or squeeze him underneath. I had no leash to tie him up. In my panic, I didn't think to leave him with a neighbor. I seized on the only option I saw: to climb over the gate with my dog in my arms.

Folks, do not try this at home, but by God's grace, I made it. I hadn't lost Morgan. He had been at risk, but I had held him fast.

God has also held me fast when I've been at risk—like the time I nearly got myself and several others killed.

I had just finished college, I was still a young Christian, and I wanted to grow in my faith. I seized a chance to work on a training program at a Christian ministry. Before I left home, I took driving lessons and my parents bought me a car.

Since few on the program had wheels, the car got plenty of use. As a brand-new driver, I was still a bit tentative and nervous. At times I let someone else take the wheel and played passenger instead. That would have been a good idea one particular day.

I didn't realize the cold medication I'd taken could affect my driving. I was leaving the ministry with a carload of people. I had to turn left onto a busy mountain highway. Thinking I had checked both ways, I hit the gas. I never noticed the car on my right, speeding toward me down the mountain.

The other driver swerved to avoid us, spinning his car toward the mountain's edge. It stopped with inches to spare. His wife and baby were inside. They could have been killed. We all could have been killed if the cars had collided. But none of us were even scratched. God surely held us fast that day—it was a miracle!

My Master kept holding me fast in the days and weeks that followed. He knew I was still in trouble. Though I was physically unharmed, my psyche was chopped liver. Guilt and horror flooded me as I thought of the carnage I had nearly caused. I sank into depression. Our mountainous setting had some drops, and I still recall gazing over the edge of one, wishing I had the guts to jump. Deep down, I knew I wouldn't go that far, but I longed to be out from under the smothering blanket of gloom that seemed as though it would never lift.

During all of this, God held me close…this time, through His people.

Caring Christians enfolded me with their prayers, encouragement, and counsel. They knew when to give me space and when to talk turkey. When the time was right, they urged me to learn from my mishap and move forward. A friend kept my car for a while, and then slowly got me back into driving—which I'd thought would never happen. Christ's body became the arms of His love. In time I healed because, though I'd lost my grip, God hadn't. He grips me still.

I kept Morgan close because I loved him. Years later, I still hold him fast. But one day death will take him from me. I am powerless to stop it. Not so my Master. He gave His Son to break death's hold on me. His Word assures me that nothing can ever separate me from His love. I am safe in His hand, and He will hold me close forever.

My sheep listen to my voice; I know them, and they follow me. I give them eternal life, and they shall never perish; no one can snatch them out of

my hand. My Father, who has given them to me, is greater than all; no one can snatch them out of my Father's hand. I and the Father are one (John 10:27-30).

Consider This

Have there been times when you were at risk and God held you fast? What did you learn about His love? His power? His faithfulness?

How might God use you as His hand to lift up someone else?

Stop, Look, and Love
Love Takes Time

Love doesn't make the world go 'round.
Love is what makes the ride worthwhile.

FRANKLIN P. JONES

When we come home in the evening and let Stuart in, he runs to each of us, jumps in our arms, and greets us. If we sit, he will leap onto our laps and lick our ears. He understands not to do this to strangers, but he knows how much each of us loves him, and he's eager to get the attention and affection he hasn't had all day.

But, I must confess, there are times when we aren't quite as eager to see Stuart as he is to see us. There are days when I'll come home and not even let him in for a few hours. Or, if he's already inside, I'll barely say hi to him, pat his head, and go off to do my own thing. It's not that I don't care. It's that the stuff of life has intruded. I'm busy and frazzled. I feel overwhelmed. I don't want to take time right then.

One such day, there had been an accident at the school where I was teaching. A student from another class hurt his leg while trying to show off. It was a serious injury, and not a pretty sight, either. The class I was teaching had seen it, and my pupils were obviously affected. I had to adjust the rest of the day to help them through their feelings. When I got home, I was physically, mentally, and emotionally exhausted.

Stuart saw me coming and jumped up and down. "Go away. I need to be alone now," I told him. He retreated and lay down in another room. I could tell from how he slumped away that he felt hurt and rejected. It made me feel terrible too, but I let him go.

A little while later, I called Stuart back. He jumped onto my lap and was all licks and wiggles. Now that I was taking time with him, he felt loved and all was well.

There have also been moments when I didn't take needed time with my children. I remember a day when my daughter Christy was quite small. We were at church, and I was talking with friends. Christy came up to tell me she'd choked on some candy, and a kind older woman had saved her. I wasn't really paying attention. "Oh, that's nice, honey. Go play," I said absently. I noticed she seemed upset when she left. But I wasn't sure why till some time later, when the woman who'd helped her told me what had happened.

Christy didn't bring it up again till we got home. Then she asked me with tears in her eyes if I'd listened when she told me Mrs. Unruh saved her life. I had to admit I'd been busy and hadn't really heard her. "I feel just awful that I didn't listen to you earlier," I said, sighing. "I'm so sorry."

Because she knew how much I loved her, she forgave me. We hugged, and she ran off happily to play.

How do I do when it comes to taking time with my heavenly Father? Am I as excited to leap into His arms as Stuart is to leap into mine? Am I willing to stop and listen when He speaks? Or do I let the stuff of life intrude on our relationship? I must confess, too often it's the latter.

Too many times I barely greet my Lord in the morning, and I often fall asleep when I talk to Him at night. There are days when I forget to open my Bible, even though I know He is eager to speak to me through it. Too often, I opt to spend time with friends or go shopping or play on the computer or veg out in front of the TV, rather than jumping into the arms of my Daddy.

Even when I am seriously into prayer, my mind may wander, drifting to something that is calling me from the outside. *What am I going to fix for dinner? What should I wear to the program?* When I catch myself, I pause, ask God's forgiveness, and continue fellowshipping with my Creator. But it's so easy for my focus to shift to my own needs. I don't take the time to love God as I should.

Love is first on Stuart's priority list. He always has time for us. He never lets the stuff of life intrude. I pray I will act on what this teaches me. I pray I will always take time to love, to be attentive to my family, and to leap into my beloved Master's arms every day of my life.

Because your love is better than life, my lips will glorify you (Psalm 63:3).

Consider This

What is the stuff of life that intrudes on your taking time to love? How does this affect your relationship with loved ones? With God? What can you do about it?

Lifted Up
God Refreshes Our Hearts

Now, God be prais'd, that to believing souls
Gives light in darkness, comfort in despair!

WILLIAM SHAKESPEARE

Toward the end of Gracie's life she was blind, deaf, and feeble in body and mind. After seizures, she'd wander the backyard, disoriented and lost, far from her food and water. This was troublesome on hot summer days. I'd find her lying in a secluded spot in the sun, panting and thirsty. When this happened, I'd lift her up, carry her into the shade, and place a dish of water beside her, which she quickly lapped up.

Reflecting on this has made me consider how my Master has often found me wandering, lost and disoriented, in the hot backyard of life. I've been panting and weary, far from spiritual food and water. And He has lifted me up.

I recall one particular morning when I woke up feeling low. I'd been busy of late, and perhaps had not spent enough time in God's Word and in prayer. Add a touch of insomnia and the usual career anxieties, and instead of facing the day with a smile, my desire was to roll myself up in a ball and hibernate until things got circum-stantially better. Maybe that's what Gracie was thinking when she curled up in the backyard, her body weary with age, her sight and hearing gone: Just lie down, give up, and wait.

But unlike Gracie, I had my sight, my hearing, and a car. I decided to drive to the mountains and take a hike. Perhaps exercise would banish the blues that clung to me like plastic wrap. However, as I walked up the hill, I realized these feelings of discouragement weren't going to leave so easily. They felt like a weight I was lugging up the mountain on my back.

I remembered a verse I had recently memorized, Jeremiah 33:3: "Call to me and I will answer you and tell you great and unsearch-able things you do not know." I had read about Bono (of the rock group U2) referring to Jeremiah 33:3 as "God's hotline." I was des-perate enough to call that number out loud. I shouted, "Okay, God. I'm calling on You. So go ahead, answer me. Tell me great and unsearchable things I do not know."

I waited a moment. I thought to myself, *I'm totally alone. There's no way I'm going to get help at this time.* I felt like Gracie: weak, disoriented, and very lost.

And then, suddenly, I heard a female voice sweetly singing that old childhood classic, "Jesus Loves Me."

A middle-aged Asian woman was making her way toward me down the mountain, singing as she went. She paused to say hello. I asked her to keep singing. She did.

As I watched her disappear down the trail, I realized God had just answered my call. He was informing me through this "angel" of a great and unsearchable thing that I didn't know a few moments ago—something I had forgotten.

Jesus loves me.

This message wasn't something I merely heard in my ears—it penetrated the depths of my heart. It reverberated, like the Liberty Bell clanging next to my head. Jesus loves me. A message so simple, yet so profound. A message I needed to hear.

That message lifted me up from the lost and disoriented place where I had wandered. It threw off my shackles of hopelessness and depression. It flooded me with love, joy, and peace. As I had lifted Gracie out of the hot sun and put her next to a bowl of cool water, God had lifted me out of the burning heat of despair, put me by His side, and given me a drink of cool, fresh, Living Water.

One of my favorite Scriptures captures the feeling of being lifted up by God: "Those who hope in the LORD will renew their strength. They will soar on wings like eagles; they will run and not grow weary, they will walk and not be faint" (Isaiah 40:31).

When you're hopelessly earthbound, to soar like an eagle is nothing short of miraculous. When Gracie was lying in the backyard, baking in the sun, too weak to move, and I lifted her up and placed her in the shade and gave her water—it was magic to her. She could never have levitated there and made the water appear on her own.

Likewise, for me to escape the gravity of despair on my own was an impossible task. But God, in His great mercy, lifted me up on wings like eagles and provided Living Water for me to drink by the power of His love.

I pray that you, being rooted and established in love, may have power, together with all the saints, to grasp how wide and long and high and deep is the love of Christ, and to know this love that surpasses knowledge—that you may be filled to the measure of all the fullness of God. Now to him who is able to do immeasurably more than all we ask or imagine, according to his power that is at work within us, to him be glory in the church and

*in Christ Jesus throughout all generations, for ever
and ever! Amen (Ephesians 3:17-21).*

Consider This

*Can you recall a time when you were feeling down and God
lifted you up? What had you been struggling with? How
did He encourage you? What did you learn about His love?
How might you use this to encourage someone else?*

Faithful to the Max
True Friends Are Forever

*I knew wherever I was that you
thought of me, and if I got in a tight
place you would come—if alive.*

WILLIAM TECUMSEH SHERMAN

It took me months to adjust when Max, our Boston terrier, passed away. When I left for work, I'd look into his corner and say, "Goodbye, Max. Have a nice day." But Max didn't occupy his corner anymore.

I learned a lot from Max over the years. He showed me what it means to be a faithful friend. It didn't matter if we were tired, wired, mad, or glad. Max was always there to meet, greet, and protect us…even after he'd gone blind.

Max stood by us in health, and especially in sickness—like the time I fell and hurt my leg so badly I couldn't walk. Max could tell how upset and frustrated I was. He stayed close, sitting by me, providing a special, quiet comfort.

He did the same for everyone. I remember when my daughter Karen got a terrible cold and fever. She lay on the living room sofa, wrapped in a blanket. Max curled up on the floor beside her for most of the day. When she put her arm down, he was there to pet.

In Max's last days, we tried to do the same for him. Those of us who were home took turns sitting beside him. He couldn't walk in the end, so we carried him outside when we thought he needed to relieve himself. My husband, Steve, was home the most, and he would faithfully change Max's blanket and keep fresh food and water near him. At night we'd say goodbye to Max and pat his head. I cried and told him I loved him, and I thanked him for a job well done.

Faithfulness is also a crown Steve wears. He, too, has been faithful in health, and especially in sickness.

On August 5, 1986, our lives changed forever. My sister and I were in a terrible car wreck. I was driving our new minivan, and I wasn't used to it. I lost control, and we went tumbling through a Nebraska field. My sister was stuck in the car, and I was thrown out. She had multiple injuries, including a leg that was broken in several places. I suffered a concussion and broke both legs, both shoulders, and my pelvis. My right leg was nearly cut off.

I was hospitalized for two weeks in Nebraska before my family could fly me home. Our church and extended family helped cook and clean, but Steve bore the brunt of caring for me. I couldn't even get to the bedroom or bathroom in my wheelchair. He had to help dress me, assist me with the porta-potty in our den, and clean the ugly wounds on my leg. He had to do every little personal thing for me that I'd always done for myself. After getting the children ready for bed, he had to get me ready too. And then, hours later, when he slept at last, I'd often feel the need to "take care of nature." Much as I hated to, I was forced to use the intercom on our phone and wake Steve up. Back he'd come to the den to take care of me. In fact, for the first few weeks, he slept on the den sofa to be near me.

He did all of this without complaining, faithfully, and with a smile.

Our son, John, was just seven when the accident happened, but he was faithful too. He decided where he belonged, and there was no discussion. He made himself a bed on the floor at the foot of mine, and curled up next to Mom.

Grateful as I was for the aid and encouragement I received from others, there were times when only one Friend could help me. God stood faithfully by me too. When the pain grew intense, when loneliness set in, when it seemed as though no one could fully understand, He was there to comfort me. At times, the physical challenge was so great that I just looked up and said, "Okay, God, it's up to You and me. Let's go."

I am so grateful for the faithfulness of Max, Steve, my children, and so many others in my life. And I am so grateful that the Lord is my most faithful Friend. I know it's a miracle that I lived. I know God has me here for a purpose. And I want to be loyal and faithful to Him as well. I hope one day, when my life here is done, I will be approved by my Master, as Max was approved by us. I hope when I get to heaven, God will take me in His arms and say, "Good job, Connie. Well done, faithful friend."

For the LORD is good and his love endures forever; his faithfulness continues through all generations (Psalm 100:5).

Consider This

What are some specific ways in which people have been faithful friends to you? How has God been your faithful Friend? How have you been a faithful friend to others and to Him? In what ways might you be more faithful still?

Love, Morgan Style
Being There Says You Care

Love is, above all, the gift of oneself.

JEAN ANOUILH

Morgan is a very empathetic little dog. If he thinks I'm upset, he tries to comfort me. He'll paw at me or lick my chin or push his face against mine. At times he'll lean his whole body against me or drape himself over me…gazing up at me with soulful brown eyes. It's his way of giving me a hug and showing me he cares.

I've seen him do this with others too. He crawled up on one friend's chest and just lay there, snuggling, sensing she was having a rough time. My dog seems to know that when someone is hurting, the most important thing he can do is be there. Of course, he has no idea what's wrong, but that doesn't stop him from reaching out. He simply offers himself.

I haven't always been as wise as Morgan…or as loving, either. Other people's pain scared me when I wasn't sure how to help. I pulled back, fearing they'd reject me if I did or said the wrong thing. In truth, I was more concerned about me than them.

But something happened with a friend of mine that changed my thinking forever. She was very upset one day, and I felt at a loss.

Instead of reaching out, I retreated. Later, we talked. She shared how wounded she was that I hadn't cared about her.

"I did care," I explained. "But I didn't know what to do."

Her next words changed my life. "Why didn't you just say that?"

She told me how much it would have meant just to know I was concerned. She told me I could have asked her how to help. I learned a great lesson that day. I don't have to have the answers; I just have to offer myself...as Morgan does.

My close friend Dottie offered herself to me last winter when my mother was gravely ill. She let me call her, sometimes several times a day. She had no answers, but she stopped her schedule, listened to me vent, prayed for me, and encouraged me from God's Word. She was my lifeline.

Jesus asked His disciples to be His lifeline when He faced the greatest crisis of His life, the cross. In the Garden of Gethsemane, He asked them to watch and pray, but they fell asleep instead. Later, when He was seized and put on trial, they retreated—all but John. John kept watch with his Lord at the foot of the cross. He couldn't change the circumstances or take Christ's pain away, but he was there. And it was to John that Jesus entrusted His mother.

Morgan tries to care and be there for me in his innocent doggie way, but he's mortal and finite. He can't be with me constantly, or always. Neither can my friends and loved ones. God can, though. In John 14:16-17, Jesus tells His disciples, "I will ask the Father, and he will give you another Counselor to be with you forever—the Spirit of truth."

God loves us, and because He cares, His Spirit is there, indwelling His children to guide, teach, and comfort us. He doesn't always remove our trials, but He is with us in them. And He wants us to do the same for each other—to be there and care in His name.

God, who comforts the downcast, comforted us by the coming of Titus, and not only by his coming but also by the comfort you had given him. He told us about your longing for me, your deep sorrow, your ardent concern for me, so that my joy was greater than ever (2 Corinthians 7:6-7).

Consider This

Has there been a time in your life when someone comforted you with their presence? How did this person minister to you? How did it make you feel loved? What effect did it have on your life, then and later?

What are some ways you might be there and care for others?

Till Death Do Us Part
Commitment Is a Choice

I meant what I said
And I said what I meant…
An elephant's faithful
One hundred per cent!

DR. SEUSS

When I was a kid, we had a dog named Poppy, aka "The Wire Haired Terrier Escape Artist." She dug under fences, squeezed through posts, shot out a door left ajar. Poppy was always trying to run away. She eventually did and never came back.

In later years my parents had a German shepherd, Ginger. Same thing—she was always waiting for an opportunity to dash to freedom. Once on the outside, she'd ignore any call to come back. It was a huge effort to track her down and bring her home.

This was not the case with Gracie. In fact, there were a number of times when I forgot to close the side gate, but the next morning Gracie was still there, lying contentedly in the backyard. Other times, she was left out in the front yard by accident, and I'd find her later, curled up on the porch, waiting for my return.

Having grown up with dogs that were born to run, it amazed and humbled me that Gracie did the opposite. I was touched by her loyalty and felt a sense of pride that I had shown her enough love and care that she *chose* to stay, when she could have easily answered the call of the wild and run off to freedom.

Gracie's loyalty reminded me of the Old Testament story of Ruth. She and another Moabite woman named Orpah lost their husbands (who were brothers, the sons of a Hebrew widow named Naomi). Naomi urged her two daughters-in-law to return to their families of origin—to find new husbands and start over—to not be burdened with an old lady like her. Orpah took the advice, but Ruth clung to Naomi and said: "Don't urge me to leave you or to turn back from you. Where you go I will go, and where you stay I will stay. Your people will be my people and your God my God. Where you die I will die, and there I will be buried. May the LORD deal with me, be it ever so severely, if anything but death separates you and me" (Ruth 1:16-17).

It was finally death that separated Gracie and me. And through all our years together, she went where I went and stayed where I stayed. She was a good and loyal dog.

As I was reading about Ruth, I was reminded that my wife read those same words of Ruth's to me on our wedding day: "May the LORD deal with me, be it ever so severely, if anything but death separates you and me." The words had great meaning to both of us. It was a pledge of faithfulness and loyalty, a pledge to stay in the yard and not run away.

In any marriage, including ours, there are many temptations and opportunities to run off to greener pastures, to slip out the gate, to dig secretly under a fence, to experience freedom from the ball and chain of daily matrimonial drudgery. We've both had times when the urge to escape each other was overwhelming. And without a physical fence to lock us in, we've had to rely on a combination of two things to keep us loyal: love for each other and love for our God.

I know how fickle feelings of love are. One moment I can feel love for my wife. Then she pushes the tiniest button and I'm ready to sail off for Tahiti, alone. I've had this happen when I'm enjoying one of my favorite pastimes—channel surfing. I'm happily manipulating the TV remote and experiencing a delightful smorgasbord of images and sounds—and suddenly Celine says, "I hate it when you do that," implying that I should stop. Tahiti, here I come!

What keeps me from running off is the love of my Lord and Master. It's because of the love and care God has shown me that I stay in the marriage (backyard) He's provided for me, even though the side gate is left open. First John 5:3 says, "This is love for God: to obey his commands." Because Celine and I made a vow not only to each other *but also to God* to stay together until death do us part—that is what we will do.

One day last year, Celine was reeling from the pressures of working part-time, getting her master's degree, and dealing with a very active two-year-old. She looked at the "filthy" kitchen I had forgotten to clean, and which *my* dog inhabited, and she had a meltdown. She wanted to escape the zoo. The negative feelings lasted a few days, during which I mopped the floor and tidied up. But the physical improvements weren't the reason Celine decided to stay. It was because we finally sat down and prayed to the One to whom we made our wedding vows.

Because we love our Master, we will obey Him; we will stay put, fence or no fence—no matter how many greener pastures and temptations come our way. In a God-centered marriage, He never fences us in. He always leaves the gate open. We can be like Poppy, Ginger, or Orpah, and choose to leave. Or we can be like Gracie and Ruth and choose to stay. But there is one thing we can be assured of—God is always faithful to us.

For the LORD will not reject his people; he will never forsake his inheritance (Psalm 94:14).

Consider This

Have you ever run away from someone or something when you really should have stayed? What happened as a result?

Have you ever made a difficult decision to be loyal and stay (because you believed you were obeying God) when every fiber of your being wanted to leave? What came of this decision?

How has your commitment to God made a difference in your relationships with others?

Scars

Love Is Costly

*My sword I give to him that shall succeed
me in my pilgrimage, and my courage
and skill to him that can get it. My
marks and scars I carry with me, to be
a witness for me, that I have fought His
battles who now will be my rewarder.*

JOHN BUNYAN

My son, John, and I were so excited when we went to get our new puppy, Stuart. The breeders were bringing him to our hometown, and we were meeting at a restaurant. We stopped at a pet store and bought special toys and food for our new dog. When we reached the restaurant, Stuart was waiting, ready to join his new family.

Or was he?

Clearly, Stuart wasn't as thrilled about us as we were about him. He seemed tired and confused. We thought it was just because he had traveled a long way. John drove home while I held him and hugged him. Stuart sat quietly as I petted him, showing next to no expression on his little puppy face. After we'd shown him around and he'd had a good meal and a nap, he started to play a bit, but he still wasn't happy.

We consulted our vet. He checked Stuart over and asked us questions about his past, but we knew nothing about his prior upbringing. The vet said Stuart appeared to have some emotional scars from his early puppyhood, but if we were patient and gave him lots of love and care, he'd get better in time. We told the vet we could handle that.

It took a few weeks of tender care, but finally Stuart seemed to realize he was loved. His personality changed from scared to playful. Still, he retained some scars of his early emotional wounds. When people clapped their hands, Stuart fled in fear. He was also afraid of forks or spoons lying in a dish on the floor. He hated the vacuum cleaner so much that he tried to chew it up anytime he was nearby when it was running. Despite our love, those scars remain to this day.

Stuart left some scars on us as well. When we held him and played with him, there were times when his razor-sharp teeth and nails sliced into our skin. Even now when I look down at my hands, I can see marks from wounds he caused. But we knew he never intended to hurt us. And we didn't scold him because we didn't want to crush his already fragile puppy spirit. So we bore his wounds out of our love for him.

At times we must bear people's wounds as well—wounds that puncture not the skin, but the heart. Years ago, I was in a wheelchair for months after a bad car wreck. Finally, I progressed to the point where I could go places, with help. Some friends were planning an outing to another city. I was slated to go. Then, one of them called and asked me to stay home. She said if I went, she'd feel obligated to push me around, and she'd really rather not. She already had enough needy people in her life; she didn't think she could handle one more. But once I was back on my feet, I was welcome to call her.

My body was still recuperating, and so were my spirit and mind. Those words hurt me deeply. I started to doubt all my friends. Did everyone feel this way about me? And if so, how would I know? Should I always stay home and not go anywhere at all?

In time my heavenly Father showed me I had some wonderful friends I could trust. But I still carried the pain of that incident with me. For months I struggled with feelings of rejection, hurt, and anger. I didn't mention it to my friend, but I prayed about it often. God told me I needed to forgive her and to ask her pardon for remaining angry with her. Finally, I took her aside privately and did so. She forgave me. And God let me know that I had to let it go, even though she never asked for my forgiveness. I had to choose not to hold the pain my friend had caused me against her any longer.

This was hard to do, though I knew that it was for my good. But she didn't realize the depth of pain she'd caused. And no matter how deep my scars might have run and how badly I'd been wounded, hadn't Jesus, my Savior, endured far more for me?

Jesus bore not just light puppy scratches, but the lashes of a leather whip and the pounding of nails into His hands and feet. He bore not the momentary, light rejection of a friend who shied away from some extra effort, but the deep rejection of the very ones He came to save. He bore the penalty for my sins, and all our sins, so we could be cleansed and have new life in Him. And even now He forgives me when I fail to spend time with Him because it's not convenient—and He doesn't hold a grudge against me—because of His sacrificial love for me.

If Jesus suffered all that for me, should I not be willing to suffer for Him; to be the arms and legs of His love? And if I am the arms and legs of His love, should I not bear some nail prints too?

To this you were called, because Christ suffered for you, leaving you an example, that you should

follow in his steps... When they hurled their insults at him, he did not retaliate; when he suffered, he made no threats. Instead, he entrusted himself to him who judges justly. He himself bore our sins in his body on the tree, so that we might die to sins and live for righteousness; by his wounds you have been healed (1 Peter 2:21, 23-25).

Consider This

Have you been deeply wounded by someone else? How has it affected you? How has it affected them? Are you still bitter, or have you forgiven the person?

Is there someone you've wounded whose forgiveness you need to ask?

First Loves

Hang On to Your First Love

He who loves God above all things
is at length the friend of God.

GOTTFRIED LEIBNITZ

Stuart loved to race through the house as a pup. He would choose a path and keep repeating it. He'd dash off across the living room, through the kitchen and den, and back into the living room once more. Then he'd leap on and off the sofa and begin all over, running the same route at top speed again and again. This special puppy behavior of Stuart's brought us much entertainment and laughter.

Stuart's older now, but from time to time he still runs a repeat path the way he used to. When this happens, it seems to be a special event for Stuart. Perhaps he's remembering and celebrating his puppyhood. In any event, it delights us to see that he hasn't entirely lost this behavior he treasured so much in his youth.

My daughter Karen has also kept something she treasured in her youth. It isn't a behavior. It's a favorite stuffed dog named Bo. Karen even took Bo along when she went to study abroad.

Since Karen's freshman year in college, her goal was to attend Oxford University in England before she graduated. To be accepted into the program, she had to meet a host of qualifications. During her junior year, she made it. So did two of her best friends.

When we said goodbye at the airport, Karen told us she was glad she'd managed to squeeze Bo into a suitcase and take him along. As a parent, I found that sweet and refreshing. A soft, stuffed toy she'd once dragged through the house, taken shopping and on family vacations, and hugged tight as she slept at night, was still special to her.

Karen later shared that taking Bo was like taking a part of home with her. Having him there with her in England helped her when she was lonely. He had been her first stuffed animal. She couldn't remember a time in her life when she hadn't loved Bo.

I can't remember a time in my life when I haven't loved Jesus. I asked Him into my heart when I was five. I still remember how excited I was and that I wanted to tell everyone about Him. I felt He was always with me, guiding and protecting me. As I grew older, my love for Him grew stronger.

Yet I know there have been times in my life when I've let other things take first place in my heart. When I was 15, I met my future husband. Though my desire was to serve my Lord, I know that for a time, my love for Steve was stronger. But after a while, I came back to God and was even more excited about my first love.

Many years later, something similar happened when we had our older daughter, Christy. She was not our first child. I'd given birth to twins prematurely. Steven lived for just two and a half hours. Erin lived 18 hours. I held Steven after he died. I held Erin as her life ebbed away, telling her what it might have been. I gave birth to Christy 11 months later.

Christy consumed me. I was concerned about every move and noise she made. I prayed so much for her and for us. I took so much time with Christy that I spent less quiet time with the Lord. For a while, she came first. But when I realized she wouldn't break, I got back to my normal self.

If Stuart and Karen had stayed children, I would have been quite disheartened. But I'm glad they kept something from childhood when they grew up. Stuart holding on to his running behavior, and Karen to her toy, show how special these first loves remain in their hearts.

Though God would have been saddened if I'd stayed a spiritual baby too, He longs for me to hold on to my first love for Him. It shows Him how special He's remained in my heart…and this pleases Him greatly.

Test me, O Lord, and try me, examine my heart and my mind; for your love is ever before me, and I walk continually in your truth (Psalm 26:2-3).

Consider This

Do you have a first love from your childhood that you still hold on to now? What is it, and what does it mean to you?

What did Christ mean to you when you first met Him? What does He mean to you now?

Swatting Flies
God Watches Over Us

Through the LORD's mercies we are not consumed,
because His compassions fail not.
They are new every morning;
great is Your faithfulness.

LAMENTATIONS 3:22-23 NKJV

During the last year of Gracie's life, she began having seizures that often left her disoriented and weak for days at a time. After a seizure, she would find a spot and lay still for hours. Usually, after resting a while, she'd be up and about. But one hot summer day, I came home to find her lying helplessly by the side of the house. Flies swarmed her relentlessly, biting her ears until they bled. When healthy, she would snap at them, puffing with pride when she caught one and eating it as though it were a delicacy. (Whenever I saw this I was reminded that my trusty companion and friend was still, indeed, a dog.)

I immediately seized my swatter and chased the flies away from Gracie. But I couldn't sit there all day and fight off these pests. I considered locking her in the sanctuary of the kitchen, but I knew she preferred the backyard. And since she lost control of her bladder and bowels for a time after seizures, it was certainly less messy to let her stay outside.

As I watched the flies swarm back to assault her, I realized how helpless she was. All she could muster up was an occasional flick of her ears. Most of the time, the bloodsuckers didn't even buzz off. If Gracie had been left alone, these unrelenting pests would have eaten her alive.

But she wasn't alone. I, her master, was there to watch over her, love her, and show her mercy. I put her inside temporarily, and then I went to the computer to search the Internet for fly repellent. There were many products available by mail, but I wanted something now. I found a recipe for a simple, homemade remedy. I followed the directions, took Gracie outside, and sprayed her with the mixture. It worked. The flies backed off.

As I watched her resting, free of pesky flies, I thought about how God loves and watches over me. I thought of how He has shown me compassion and mercy when I was helpless and unable to defend myself.

Not long before the fly incident with Gracie, I was driving to a business meeting, feeling weary and defeated. Just as her seizures sapped her strength, I occasionally had attacks of self-doubt that paralyzed my creativity. *What if so-and-so doesn't like my writing? Will I ever work again? Have I lost my muse?*

This particular day, swarms of fears and doubts had been buzzing around me like flies. I couldn't shake them. I had also forgotten an appointment, and it nagged at me. It made me feel stupid, on top of all the other negative vibes that sucked my lifeblood that night. I felt helpless, like Gracie, and thought there was nothing I could do to get rid of these pests. There were just too many of them.

As I drove over Beverly Glen, a winding pass through the mountains from the San Fernando Valley to the west side of Los Angeles, I gave in—there was nothing I could do but suffer. There was no magic pill in my glove compartment, no self-help mantra I could chant to take away my blues.

And then, a tiny voice in my mind told me God was watching over me. Even though I'm not a crier, I began to tear up just a little. There was mist in my eyes. I started to sing "Jesus Loves Me" in a last-ditch effort to make the pain go away. Just as I finished the song, I looked up. A magnificent rainbow stretched across the sky, one of the most beautiful I have ever seen. It reached from one side of the valley to the other. It snapped me from depression to joy and sent my spirits soaring. God showered me with His love, chasing off the flies of doubt, fear, and hurt. It was doubly amazing when I recalled that the rainbow was a sign God gave Noah, a beautiful visual reminder of His promise never to flood the earth again. I sensed a promise in it for me too—that God would never allow me to drown in my own doubts and fears. No matter where I was— driving in my car or lying in my backyard covered with flies—He would never forsake me.

In a twinkling I had experienced God's great compassion, mercy, and love. He watches over me as I watched over Gracie— but with a bright flame of perfection beside which my feeble efforts are but a flicker. What an incredible assurance that when I come to the end of my power, when I'm lying helpless by the side of the road (like the fellow beaten by robbers in the tale of the Good Samaritan found in Luke 10:25-37), God knows and cares. He never lets me out of His sight. Just as Gracie would never have had the insight or ability to access the Internet, read directions in English, buy and mix ingredients, and spray herself with a mixture that could bring her relief…I could not in a million years have conjured up a *rainbow*. I could not have guessed how a perfectly timed arc of color in the sky would heal my soul and banish my spiritual flies. But God, in His wisdom, did. And He applied a remedy that was beyond my human comprehension.

Just as Gracie couldn't dream or imagine all the ways I loved and cared for her, I can't dream or imagine all the ways my Master cares for me. His mercy and love are eternal. He will bless my soul forever.

As a father has compassion on his children, so the LORD has compassion on those who fear him (Psalm 103:13).

Consider This

Can you think of a time when you felt so down and out that all you could do was cry out to God for mercy? Did you feel He answered? In what way did He minister to you?

How might you be used of God as a Good Samaritan to show His love, compassion, and mercy to someone else in need?

Doggie Doldrums and Their Cure

Encourage One Another

If thou knewest thy sins, thou
wouldst lose heart.

Blaise Pascal

After Steve and I had been married for a year, we moved back to our hometown of Bakersfield and got our first puppy. McPherson was a German shepherd/Australian shepherd mix. He was born on Steve's parents' farm. Before we got him, he'd lived in a cotton trailer—a trailer used to transport freshly picked cotton to the cotton gin for cleaning. Steve's parents put a blanket in one of their trailers and kept McPherson's mom and her puppies there, where it was clean and safe.

McPherson had a lot to learn…and so did we. Though both Steve and I had pets as kids, we'd never been adult pet owners. As we began to train our new dog, we made a major parenting mistake. Whenever McPherson did something wrong, we yelled at him: "Bad dog, McPherson!" Because he was young and untrained, McPherson heard "bad dog" a lot.

Like all puppies, McPherson loved to chew. Once, he chewed on Steve's work boots until he put a hole in one. We scolded him and showed him the shoe and told him he was a bad boy. He looked at us with his big, brown puppy eyes and slunk away.

Another time I was trying to bake a special pie for Steve. McPherson jumped up at the table and swiped the mixing bowl with his paw. What I'd envisioned as a beautiful pie became a mess of sticky, sweet apples splattered all across the kitchen floor. Again, I yelled at McPherson: "Bad dog!" He wanted to lick up the fruit, but I threw the back door open and shooed him outside.

Poor McPherson heard those horrible words, "bad dog," much more than he heard "good dog." We yelled at him a lot more than we hugged him. It didn't take long for his little puppy spirit to be broken. He didn't play with us as much. He didn't look us in the eyes with his puppy smile the way he had before.

We finally realized we were doing things wrong and asked others for advice. They told us not to yell at McPherson and to give him more praise. He needed to hear "good dog" to know what he was doing right. He needed to get more approval than correction, and he needed our correction to be gentle.

We took the advice, and it lifted McPherson out of his doggie doldrums. Soon, he was running and jumping and joyful again. He could see and hear that we loved him. He knew he was a "good dog."

Like McPherson, we can lose heart if we're overwhelmed by our mistakes. Wise parents, and bosses, train their charges with this truth in mind. My friend and coauthor, Marion Wells, experienced this on her first job after college.

She had gone to work for a ministry where she could also be nurtured in her fledgling Christian faith. She was put to work typing letters. Her typing had previously been confined to term papers, and her skills in this area left a bit to be desired.

If she typed five letters in a morning, she would normally get three back to redo. Naturally, this felt discouraging to her. But her superior urged her to keep at it, believing she would improve with time. He also prayed for her. Eventually, things turned around, and she became a valued employee.

It was not until a year later that she learned a startling truth. All five letters she'd typed had had to be redone. But her boss had given two to the other secretary so as not to crush Marion's spirit.

Our heavenly Master understands that we would be overwhelmed and crushed if we knew the full extent of our sins all at once. He knows that, like McPherson, I'd lose heart if all I heard was, "Bad girl, Connie." I am grateful that His Spirit is refining me bit by bit. I am thankful that when He shows me a fault, He is also at work in me to correct it, if I will cooperate with Him. And I am heartened that my Master is quick to praise me in His still, small voice: "Good girl, Connie!"

I am also aware that I can get ahead of God in other people's lives and show them their faults before He would have done so. I know that before I speak, I must pray and seek His leading about whether to share, and when, and how.

Peter must have been terribly crushed in spirit after he denied Christ three times before His crucifixion, as the Lord had predicted. Jesus knew. He didn't say, "Bad boy, Peter" or "I told you so." He appeared to Peter after His resurrection, graciously restored him, and commissioned him to "Feed my sheep" (John 21:17).

Isn't it wonderful that our God is a God of encouragement?

For this is what the high and lofty One says—he who lives forever, whose name is holy: "I live in a high and holy place, but also with him who is contrite and lowly in spirit, to revive the spirit of

the lowly and to revive the heart of the contrite"
(Isaiah 57:15).

Consider This

What are some important ways others have encouraged you? How has God encouraged you? How might you encourage someone else?

Center of Attention
Focus on God

*My only regret in the theater is that I
could never sit out front and watch me.*

JOHN BARRYMORE

When I was single, the only other living thing I had to worry about besides myself was Gracie. I had ample time to spend on her care, feeding, and entertainment. When visitors dropped in, Gracie was often the center of attention. She was a cute, friendly dog, and I showed her off like a precious child. I'd dress her up in a Hawaiian-style doggie scarf and visor. I taught her how to break dance. She'd roll over on her back, and I'd spin her on the hardwood floor. I told people she could do comic impressions of other dog breeds. I smushed her face so it took on the loose-skinned look of a Shar-Pei. I lifted her floppy ears, and she was a German shepherd. I squeezed her ears into points and pulled her skin back, and Gracie resembled a Doberman.

For many years, Gracie was my pride and joy—Daddy's little girl.

Then I got married and had a son.

Gracie was still my best dog pal, but she wasn't the only living thing I had to take care of anymore. My wife and I were now wrapped up in taking care of this helpless little human being God had entrusted into our care.

All Skye had to do was smile—or cry—to become the center of attention. He became the one we dressed up in Hawaiian shirts. He'd be the one to entertain our visitors with his infectious laughter or his wobbly attempts to walk. I still spent quality time with Gracie and took care of all her needs, but my primary passion had shifted to my son.

This got me thinking about where my focus was in my pre-Gracie, pre-God life. If I'm honest, I was wrapped up in myself. As a confirmed bachelor and seeker of pleasures and entertainment, my universe definitely revolved around…ME.

One particular area of self-gratification was collecting collectibles—cool things I acquired to shine the spotlight of attention on yours truly. I collected vintage cars: Corvette, Chevy Nomad, Mustang, Studebaker Golden Hawk, Austin Healey 3000, Mercedes 190-SL. I stockpiled jukeboxes—Wurlitzer 1015 (colored lights and bubbles), a 1954 Seeburg 100-R (*Happy Days'* style), AMI "Mother of Plastic"—among half a dozen others. Add in old pinball machines, slot machines, and a garage full of old arcade machines, and you get the rather cluttered picture.

It was an obsession, a way to draw attention to myself and give myself a snazzy identity (the fun guy with the cool cars and jukeboxes). But just as my son's arrival moved Gracie out of first place—the arrival of God's Son in my life knocked me off center stage. My life became less about me and more about Him.

The more I worshipped Christ, and the more He became the center of my attention, the less my material objects meant to me. My need-to-be-cool factor decreased as my faith factor increased. The energy I put into seeking and acquiring the temporary things of this world and my own glory was now being transferred into seeking and acquiring the unseen and eternal things of God. Of course, it wasn't an overnight change, and I'll be undergoing withdrawal symptoms for the rest of my life. I've sold all my cars, cut down on the jukeboxes, and packed away most of those other collectibles in my garage—hoping to one day get up the courage to sell them on eBay.

If we seek God diligently, He will prioritize all aspects of our lives by His wisdom and love. It's not wrong to collect cars, jukeboxes, and pinball machines; to love our children; to adore our pets. But it is wrong to have other gods before Him.

God is the only One who rightfully should be the center of our attention.

Jesus replied: "Love the Lord your God with all your heart and with all your soul and with all your mind. This is the first and greatest commandment" (Matthew 22:37-38).

Consider This

If your life is a target with a bull's-eye in the center—what do you put in that all-important high-scoring central spot? How would you label the other, lesser-scoring rings of the target? If God is not your center of attention, why isn't He?

Splashes of Blessing
Soak Up God's Goodness

Praise God, from whom all blessings flow!
Praise Him, all creatures here below!
Praise Him above, ye heavenly host!
Praise Father, Son, and Holy Ghost!

THOMAS KEN

One lovely Sunday afternoon my sister-in-law had our family over for a birthday party and swim. She invited Stuart to come too so he could romp with her two basset hounds, Willie and Jackson.

After lunch, we changed into our suits. As we were playing in the pool, Stuart started racing around it at top speed. He stopped at one end, put his paws on the pool's edge, and looked at us, longing to join us. But he'd never been swimming before. He was scared. "Come on, Stuart. Jump," we called, trying to encourage him. But he couldn't quite do it.

Stuart kept on running from one end of the pool to the other, planting his paws, staring at us, straining to overcome his fears. We could see that his desire was to be with the family he loved. We could have intervened, but we wanted him to jump into the pool by himself. This went on for about half an hour.

Willie and Jackson watched Stuart with great interest, yet it was quite evident that jumping into the pool was something *they* had no intention of doing.

Then, suddenly, Stuart took the plunge. When he got wet, we could tell he was nervous and scared. He was in unfamiliar territory, and he wasn't in control. But he was with us. He had achieved his goal.

"Good dog, Stuart," we shouted. He showed us his puppy smile and swam toward us as we swam toward him. When we connected, we hugged him and took him to a step where he could stand and still be in the water. (Dogs can drown in a pool if they don't know how to find and use the steps in the shallow end, so be sure to teach them and renew the lesson periodically so they don't forget. And they shouldn't ever be near a pool unsupervised.) Stuart stood with us for a little while, soaking up our praise and attention. Then he climbed out and lay on the grass. He seemed quite satisfied with himself, and we were proud of him too, for finding the courage to receive the goodness we offered.

Like Stuart, sometimes I must take a plunge to soak up the goodness God wants to give me. I recall going on a missions trip to Japan in my late teens. It had been hot and miserable for days. When it started to rain, I went for a walk in the downpour with a fellow from our group.

I'll never forget it. I was young and single and with a great-looking guy. We watched the locals dash inside the buildings or pull out umbrellas to shelter themselves from the deluge. We could have run from it too, but we stood there together, heads lifted high, arms outstretched, laughing as our Father soaked us from head to toe with His goodness. It was fun to see people's reactions. We imagined what they must be thinking. *Look at those crazy Americans! What will they do next?*

But that's how we chose to accept the rain—with joy, as a gift from our Father. He desires to give us so many wonderful blessings.

Sometimes I hang back, like Stuart did, because I am afraid or I want to be in control. But He wants us to trust Him and receive what He offers, as our ten-year-old granddaughter did recently when she got baptized.

Sierra joined our family when her mother, Sari, married our son John. She has added great sunshine and Son-shine to our lives. She has gone to church all her life and accepted Christ as her Savior years ago. But she'd never been baptized.

In our children's church, Sierra heard what it meant to be baptized and follow Jesus. She was eager to do this and to share her testimony. She talked to Sari and John, and together they went to our pastor. He gladly welcomed her into the baptism class.

Sierra was beaming from head to toe when she told us about it. Not only would she be baptized, but our son, John, would be in the water with her to assist the pastor. John seemed just as excited as Sierra. He felt so honored to be part of this special event in her life.

Sierra's grandparents made a two-hour trip to be present at the ceremony. Our whole family was there as well. Watching John and Sierra walk into the baptistery was incredible. The walls seemed to glow with happiness and joy. John held Sierra as she shared what Jesus meant to her, then he gently lowered her into the water at the appropriate moment. When she came up, the church applauded loudly.

Several children were baptized that day. The room was filled with praise to our awesome heavenly Father. We knew God was with us, smiling.

Just like Stuart at the pool, and like me in Japan, Sierra had a decision to make. She could choose to receive her Master's blessings, or she could hang back. When she lifted her arms to soak up His presence, she was bathed in His joy.

Heart to Heart   59

Praise be to the God and Father of our Lord Jesus Christ, who has blessed us in the heavenly realms with every spiritual blessing in Christ (Ephesians 1:3).

Consider This

Is there a blessing God wants to give you that you're hesitant to receive? Why are you hanging back? What might help you take the plunge? What might you gain by doing so?

Close to You
Draw Near to God

*Think of God more frequently
than you breathe.*

EPICTETUS

"Close to You" is a pop song from the '60s made famous by the Carpenters. It's about the sweet longing someone has to be near his or her special loved one. For Gracie, I was that special person: the center of her universe, the guy around whom her whole life revolved. As far as I could tell, the best place in the world for her to be—where she felt the most comfortable, content, and loved—was close to me, her loving master and friend.

Gracie demonstrated this desire by her actions. She consistently did everything she could to be close to me. When I was writing, Gracie would curl up on the rug beneath the table and wait for me to take her for a walk. When I was cooking in the kitchen, she'd park herself next to the stove and watch me, perhaps waiting for a scrap to fall on the floor. When I read the paper in the backyard, she'd often nap with her head resting on my foot. If I had allowed it, she would have slept in my bed every night, ridden shotgun in my truck every time I drove, and sat next to me in church every Sunday morning. It didn't matter where or when—this dog longed to be close to me.

My wife and I desire to be close to each other in our marriage. But when I'm angry with her or she's feeling hurt by me, we can live in the same house, drive in the same car, sit beside each other in church, even sleep in the same bed—and still be *emotionally* miles apart. It's not until we talk things out, make up, and pray, that our closeness is restored. Just as Gracie took daily action to get close to me, I must take daily action to get close to Celine. It may mean remembering to wash the floor, giving her a hug and kiss when I leave the house, holding hands when we take a walk, or initiating prayer together at the end of the day. It's often hard work because neither one of us is as unconditionally loving and consistent in our desire to be close to each other as Gracie was about being close to me. We have work, a son, friends, family, and separate interests to distract us from one another.

Then, there's my longing to be close to God, my loving Master and Friend. I know that the best place in the world to be—where I *should* feel the most comfortable, content, and loved—is close to Him. So why, I ask myself, am I not as single-minded as my dog? Why don't I spend the largest part of my day trying to be close to God? Yes, I have family, friends, a career, and other interests to distract me—but I think the main reason pursuing closeness with God is challenging is because God is invisible and only perceived by faith. He's not some guy sitting in my backyard, reading the paper. I can't nuzzle up to Him and rest my head on His lap. He's not my spouse—the first person I see in the morning when I awake. God is spirit and we are flesh. He cannot be seen by mere human eyes or heard with mere human ears.

According to Scripture, if we have received Christ, the Spirit of God lives in us. How much closer can we get to God than that? He lives inside us and promises to never leave or forsake us. And yet, just as Gracie and I could be physically apart, as Celine and I could be emotionally apart—there are times when I feel spiritually apart from God because of sin.

Paul talks about his struggle to remain close to God in Romans 7:22-23: "For in my inner being I delight in God's law; but I see another law at work in the members of my body, waging war against the law of my mind and making me a prisoner of the law of sin at work within my members."

When the Holy Spirit convicts me of sin (which is more often than I'd like to admit), I feel distant from God. And like Gracie wanting to be physically close to me, and Celine and I wanting to be emotionally close to each other, I must take certain actions to restore my spiritual closeness with God.

One of my favorite ways to get back into close relationship with God was to hike in the mountains with Gracie. I'd find an especially convicting portion of Scripture and write it on the back of an old business card. While I hiked, I'd take out this card and memorize the verses. As I prayed, confessed my sin, and meditated on the truth, I'd look out at the beautiful mountains. In that natural setting, with no visible signs of modern life (cars, streets, or buildings), I'd suddenly feel as though I could have been walking 2000 years ago in the company of Christ. As I walked with the "Word," the verses I was memorizing took on deeper and deeper meanings. It was like clicking icons on a computer and having screen after screen open up. The "sin gap" that made me feel distant from God was closed as this took place. Through spending quiet time with God, in His Word and in prayer, I was once again close to Him.

Gracie had her ways to get close to me. Celine and I have our ways to get close to each other. We, as children of God, have His assurance that He is always close to us. For once we open the door and accept Christ into our hearts, God promises that nothing can ever separate us from His love.

For I am convinced that neither death nor life, neither angels nor demons, neither the present nor the future, nor any powers, neither height nor depth, nor anything else in all creation, will be able to separate us from the love of God that is in Christ Jesus our Lord (Romans 8:38-39).

Consider This

When have you felt closest to God? When have you felt farthest away? What action do you personally take to get closer to Him when you feel distant?

Have you received Jesus Christ as your Savior and Lord? If so, can you be assured that nothing will be able to separate you from God's love?

Fairy Dogfather

Will You Be a "Fool" for God's Love?

*Wisdom and folly, if pushed far
enough, kick into each other.*

AUTHOR UNKNOWN

If you've ever read fairy tales, you've heard of fairy godmothers. They're those magical creatures who fly to the rescue just when our hero or heroine seems doomed. They fix impossible situations with a wave of their magic wands and turn a troubled world right side up.

Well, we don't have one of those, but our dog Stuart is Steve's "fairy dogfather."

My dear husband is a hardworking farmer. He comes home tired and dirty from his long days. Many times he feels frustrated too. He has to fix tractors and other farm equipment. It's often hard to find the right part or figure out what's gone wrong in the first place. When he drags himself through the door, he just wants to slump into his recliner and rest.

Stuart has another idea. He flies (okay, leaps) onto Steve's lap and starts licking my husband's ears. He goes from one ear to the next, wiggling and jumping. Soon Steve is laughing and hugging

Stuart. Maybe Stuart can't fix Steve's situation, but his antics magically lift Steve's spirits and turn his troubled mood right side up.

Without realizing it, our precious dog is being a "fool for love." He doesn't know or care if licking Steve's ears seems silly. He just knows he loves his master unconditionally, and his reckless affection is just the right magic to gladden Steve's heart.

I also had a chance to play such a role…to engage in some seemingly silly antics that might lift people's spirits and point them to God's love. My friend Susie and I wrote a skit to promote a women's retreat. Her character was a stressed, tired woman who was in great need of a break from her heavy life load. Everything she saw, thought, said, and felt was negative. I was her "fairly reliable fairy godmother," who showed up smiling, full of good wishes and cheer, and wearing a tutu and wings.

Our goal was to publicize the retreat with a goofy character who'd make people laugh, while helping them realize how foolish it would be to rely on such a silly source of help when they had a heavenly Father to turn to, who loved them and had life's real answers.

Creating the fairy godmother costume was quite a job. A friend's huge white petticoat that she wore square dancing worked great as a tutu. Another friend lent me a blouse. I bought some wonderfully large wings, and we made a magic wand.

Stuart sat and watched while we practiced the skit, as if he was giving his approval. At one point we nearly gave up, thinking it wouldn't work. Stuart saw my frustration and jumped onto my lap, doing his "fairy dogfather" ear licking routine, as if to cheer me up.

When it came time to perform the skit, it took several friends to get me into my outfit, fix my hair, and do my makeup. But looking a bit silly was well worth it. We heard some were touched by the unhappy woman and how she was helped, and others laughed for the first time all week. I didn't mind being a "fool for love" if I'd helped point people to God's unconditional love.

And He was a "fool for love" too…at least from a strictly human perspective.

God the Son laid aside His glory to become a humble servant and be born into the world as a human being. When He brought His message, He was laughed at not in delighted fun, but with scorn and ridicule. And He suffered and died for the very ones who were rejecting Him. Sounds silly, humanly speaking, doesn't it?

But God's wisdom often seems silly to our human minds. Jesus' reckless affection worked. He obtained His goal. He paid for our sins. He lifted us out of them into God's family, if we have believed in Him. He lifts our hearts and spirits now, and one day we'll be raised in resurrection, to spend eternity with Him.

Stuart doesn't mind being a "fool for love" with his family. I didn't mind looking a bit silly to a friendly audience. But am I willing to be a "fool for love" like Jesus was? Am I willing to look silly by sharing the gospel with those who might ridicule me for it? Am I willing to show His kind of reckless affection? Am I willing to suffer persecution to share His unconditional love, so that others might find the One who is always reliable, and so much more than a fairy godmother?

God calls us to be "fools" for His love—and that's not silly at all!

For the message of the cross is foolishness to those who are perishing, but to us who are being saved it is the power of God (1 Corinthians 1:18).

Consider This

Have you ever felt silly when sharing the gospel? What made you feel that way? How do you think God viewed the situation?

Is God nudging you to tell someone about Him and be a "fool for love"?

What's in a Name?

Our Master Has Renamed Us

What signifies knowing the Names,
if you know not the Natures of Things.

Benjamin Franklin

Gracie had a checkered past. I don't know exactly when or where she was born. I don't know who her original owners were—only that someone had abandoned her in a parking lot, nameless and untagged. That's where a friend of a friend found her, starving and with a gash over one of her eyes. This Good Samaritan brought the future Gracie to her vet, paid to have her cut stitched up, and named her Short Stuff. She welcomed Short Stuff into her home, but one of her other dogs didn't think it was such a good idea. They fought often. That's where I came in.

I had been praying about getting a dog. As a long-term bachelor, I thought it was about time to introduce a living thing into my life—something I'd have to be responsible for. But I had my fears. Would a dog be too dirty and noisy? Would it impinge on my social life and travels? The thought of choosing and committing to the right dog began to bring up familiar feelings of anxiety. This could be as difficult as choosing the right mate.

During the first week of thinking about getting a dog, I told a few friends of my intentions. One of them suggested we pray about it. I said I'd envisioned a weenie dog or something like that. We put it to God. We'd no sooner finished praying than the phone rang.

Another pal to whom I'd casually mentioned my dog interest was calling to inform me about a weenie-like tan dog named Short Stuff. The pooch was a 20-minute drive away. Would I like to come and see her now? I said yes, and off I went.

As soon as I entered the house, a chunky shepherd-corgi mix (imagine a Eureka canister vacuum cleaner with legs) barreled around the corner and rushed up to me. She licked my hands as if they were basted with meat sauce, her tail wagging fast enough to propel a boat. The interim owner said Short Stuff was never that friendly to males before. (She suspected the dog was once beaten by a man.) Not taking that as a dig to my masculinity, but as the compliment it was meant to be, I decided to take Short Stuff home with me that very day.

On the drive back, I thanked God for how easy He had made it. I didn't have to look at any other dogs. My new mutt was house-broken and instantly took to my yard. She found a cozy spot to sleep in the kitchen, and I installed a doggie door so she could go in and out as she pleased. Both she and I knew she was home. Now, the only thing left to deal with was her name…Short Stuff.

Although it was cute, the name seemed demeaning and redundant, like calling a short guy "Shorty" or a Caucasian person "Whitey." But more than that, the name didn't match the dog I knew God had given to me as a gift. Short Stuff only described the external dog. I wanted a name that described her spirit and heart.

A verse came to mind that I had read earlier in the week: "God opposes the proud but gives grace to the humble" (James 4:6). Grace is a gift from God…and this dog was also a gift. I felt rather humble about it too. I usually research things to death before I make a decision. The way I've shopped for cars, electronics, and a wife, it's a wonder I've attained any of these things in this lifetime.

Grace is undeserved favor. As I quickly came to know my dog, it became apparent she was grace. How could a selfish guy like me end up with such a terrific little mutt? It was undeserved! And God had blessed me with a dog who actually gave me more than I gave her. That was favor!

Now the only issue was whether to call her Grace or Gracie. One good look at her answered my question. Gracie had a shepherd head stuck on a corgi-esque body with stubby little legs. Once, I took her walking on the Venice Beach boardwalk in Southern California, an area known for colorful and often bizarre characters (chainsaw jugglers, tattoo artists, bikini-clad skaters). But Gracie was the one getting all the stares and comments: "Oh, what a funny dog!" "How oddly cute!" "What kind of dog *is* that?"

This dog was no elegant, stuffy, prim-and-proper lady named Grace. This dog was humorous, amusing, a little goofy, and proud of it (like that wonderful comedienne Gracie Allen). That was Gracie!

So what about Kris? What was I before God found me, a stray soul wandering abandoned and abused in the parking lot of life? Without getting into my whole life story, I was an insecure, selfish, fearful guy who tried his best to be cool by surrounding himself with a plethora of cool people and things that masked the real me—a less-than-cool person that I became aware of while lying awake in bed between three and four in the morning.

But when God invited me into a relationship with Him, and I said yes, I took on a new identity, and He gave me a new name. According to my driver's license, my name is still Kris. But when you check my spiritual dog tag, it is engraved "Child of God." My new name brings with it all the perks of having a Master who cares about and loves me, a Master who protects me under the shadow of His wings and provides all my needs.

I'm so thankful that I, who was lost like Gracie, have now been found, and to prove it, I have a new name!

How great is the love the Father has lavished on us, that we should be called children of God! And that is what we are! (1 John 3:1).

Consider This

What names have others given you? How did they affect your self-image? If they were negative, have you broken free of those old labels, or do they still haunt you?

What other names, besides child of God, are bestowed on those who belong to the Lord? How do these names describe your new identity in Christ?

Divine Dog Tags
Our True Identity Is in Christ

*O Lord, you have searched
me and you know me.*

Psalm 139:1

Max was a Boston terrier. Some folks thought he was ugly, but we thought otherwise. He was small, about 15 pounds, and he had a nice black-and-white coat. Like all Boston terriers, Max's eyes were wide apart and bugged out. When he stared straight ahead, people on both his right and left thought he was looking at them. In his later years, our mama cat attacked Max and cut his eye. This left one eye white and blind and gave him a somewhat distinctive appearance.

Ugly or not, Max's identity didn't come mainly from his looks. It came from his unique personality and from being ours. Everyone in our area knew who Max was and that he was owned by the Fleishauers. Occasionally, he got lost. Someone always brought him back. He belonged to us. We belonged to him. No questions asked!

That was some years ago. Now our little farming community has turned into a new-home neighborhood. With so many houses being built and new people coming in, we don't all know each other the way we once did. Max has passed away, but I've wondered what would happen if he got lost today. What if his dog tags were old and faded, and whoever found him couldn't read them? If they had to depend on the tags to identify him, they would not know who he was.

Humans have dog tags too. They're called fingerprints. They help prove our identity to those who don't know us. I had to be fingerprinted to be cleared to be a substitute teacher. Even though my old prints were on file because I'd taught before, a new set was required.

I went down to the county school administration office. The lady who did fingerprinting rolled my right thumb over a little screen. My print was projected on the screen. Soon after, a sign popped up. It said "reject."

The woman tried my other thumb and got the same response: a little banner across my unique print. "Reject." She patiently took the prints of the other four fingers from both hands. She kept on getting the same signs: "reject" or "no match."

By now I was getting just a bit nervous, so she kindly explained that sometimes fingerprints become worn or faint when a person grows older. I said I would be happy to provide a sample of my hair for DNA, but she wasn't amused. She just kept repeating the process. Finally she said she was giving up. Out of all the prints she took, she got only one good thumb print. She just hoped it would be enough.

I walked out of the building completely stunned. There were lots of things on my body I'd worried about, but I'd never given my fingerprints a second thought. Now they were fading. What did this mean?

Crazy thoughts came to mind. I could rob a bank and no one could identify me. (Yeah, right!) If I were mangled in a car wreck, no one could identify me. I'd failed a lot of tests in my life…but my own identity?

I reflected on the fact that I've changed in other ways over the years. For instance, I've added many pounds to my body. I've often said, tongue in cheek, "I'm twice the woman I used to be." Yet people from my past still recognize me, if not by my looks, then by my voice or smile.

I kept fretting, still rather wrapped up in myself. Then, as my heavenly Father often does, He thumped me on the head and said, "Connie, think about Me." So I did. And I realized my true identity was in Christ.

I have given my heart and life to Christ, and God has sealed me with His divine dog tag, the presence of His Spirit within me. That tag was purchased for me with Christ's blood. No matter what I accomplish in this lifetime, no matter where I succeed or fail, no matter who I know or what I say, what counts most is that I belong to Him.

No matter how Max's looks changed as he aged, no matter how his tags faded, whether others recognized him or not, he was still ours, and we knew him and loved him.

No matter how much I've changed through the years, regardless of whether my fingerprints print, I am God's child, and He knows and loves me too.

I am the good shepherd; I know my sheep and my sheep know me (John 10:14).

Consider This

What do you think friends and family see as your true identity? What do coworkers see? What do strangers see? What does God see? How are they different?

Gracie Looks
at the Heart
God Sees Who We Are Inside

Beauty comes from within.

PROVERB

Have you ever considered the difference between how you see yourself, how your dog sees you, and how God sees you? I have, and I've found it quite revealing. Viewing myself through Gracie's eyes has reminded me of God's perspective…which doesn't always match up with my own.

Some days I wake up on the wrong side of the bed. Perhaps I've tossed and turned all night, sleepless from a myriad of worries ranging from financial woes to marriage friction, parenting frustrations, or even fears such as, "Is that a sore muscle in my hand or the first twinges of rheumatoid arthritis?"

I get up and look in the mirror. Unbelievable! Who is that old man staring back at me? I see more white hair than before, but less hair overall. My face seems tired, as though it's made of wax and drooping on a hot day. And is that mark a freckle or an age spot? At least I have contact lenses now. Before they came to my rescue, I had to endure those thick pop-bottle glasses I'd worn since childhood—haunting my face like an ever-present spirit of embarrassment and shame.

My eyes rove down to my body. The bicycle tire around my waist is itching to graduate to an automobile tire. I now favor wearing my shirt out (the Hawaiian casual look), not so much for style but because my pants are tight. I don't want to call attention to the flab that's bulging over my waist like over-yeasted homemade bread. Okay, so most of my pals think I'm one of the leaner people they know, and they keep telling me all this bodily decline stuff is in my head, but they can't see the way I feel!

All this is just the physical, the tip of the iceberg. What's beneath the surface is my frustration at not having achieved all I wanted to by this age. My youthful goals that were in the "realm of possibility" are now jettisoning away—like an astronaut cut of his tether line—sucked away into deep space, growing smaller and smaller, just a dot now, soon to be forever lost in the void.

Yes, on these particular days, from where I'm standing, from my uniquely ME point of view, I look and feel like a failure. Unlovable is an understatement. I'm the raggedy and ripped stuffed animal you can't even give away to the Salvation Army—that the dog won't even play with. I feel as photogenic—and confident—as a smashed snail. I probably have bad breath too, and I just don't know it. I want to crawl into a hole or be cast away on a deserted island where I can grow ugly, old, and insignificant in peace.

Okay—you get the picture. We all have days like that, don't we? (At least I hope we do, because misery loves company.) And on those days, especially before I was married, I'd still have to go out and feed Gracie her morning meal.

Gracie didn't seem to see what I saw in that mirror. Even on those mornings, unless she was sick, she'd bound up to me, tail wagging so furiously she could take off and fly, jumping with the fervor of a groupie in the presence of her favorite rock star. Never once did she appear to look down on me for my unkempt, ugly, unseemly, less-than-movie-star appearance. She didn't walk a big critical circle around me and go, "Whoa! Check out the hangdog, insecure countenance of this guy. Who is this disgusting excuse for a human being?" No, Gracie never cared how I looked on the outside. All she saw was her beloved master. At least, that's how she made me feel.

I must say, there were times when the unconditional love of this dog made all the difference in how I went on with my day. Gracie didn't look at the external me. She was only concerned about my heart. She kept giving me the same wake-up call: *Your outer man isn't nearly as important as your inner man.* Gracie loved me for who I really was, not who I felt I was at a particular given moment. She focused on my essence, the "me" God created to last forever.

In 1 Samuel 16:7 we read, "The LORD said to Samuel, 'Do not consider his appearance or his height, for I have rejected him. The LORD does not look at the things man looks at. Man looks at the outward appearance, but the LORD looks at the heart.'" When I think about this, the message of this verse truly lifts my head and fills me with joy. How Gracie perceived me on this earth—this simple dog who did not consider my outward appearance but looked at my heart—was a foreshadowing, a glimpse of the incredible way my heavenly Father perceives me.

It amazes me how God used Gracie to teach me this basic truth—that what makes me lovable and worthy isn't my external body that decays with each tick of the clock. My self-worth shouldn't be measured by the amount of love and approval I receive from other people based on how they rate the accessories and accoutrements adorning my outer man. No, it is my heart, the internal, eternal part of me, which defines who I am.

God sees that…and so do our dogs.

*Now we see in a mirror, dimly, but then face to face.
Now I know in part, but then I shall know just as
I also am known (1 Corinthians 13:12 NKJV).*

Consider This

Do you see others as God does, or as man does? What message does this send? How might you adjust your focus to be more in line with God's?

The Master's Door
God Made a "Door" for Us

Heaven-gates are not so highly arch'd
As princes' palaces; they that enter there
Must go upon their knees.

JOHN WEBSTER

Before I got Gracie, the thought crossed my mind that owning a dog would be too much trouble. I was happy with my bachelor life. I had no worries about feeding or caring for anyone else except me. But I decided I wanted a dog. I prayed for one. And along came Gracie…a gift from God.

I took her in, fed her, provided fresh water, and combed her for fleas. Then I had to figure out where she would sleep. I, her master, had to decide how much of my house and life to share with her.

Gracie wasn't a big dog. Short legs, belly slung like an occupied hammock, she had a shepherd head on a compact corgi body. Where I lived, the weather could go to extremes (for Southern California). It could get very cold at night and quite hot in the daytime. I knew Gracie would be more comfortable inside when that happened. We also had coyotes and rattlesnakes in the neighborhood, and mountain lions had been spotted in the area. Since Gracie came housebroken and wasn't a heavy shedder, I began to consider installing a doggie door in the kitchen so she could go in and out as she pleased.

This went against my entire upbringing. As a child, we always had dogs, mostly German shepherds because my father was partial to them. But they always stayed outdoors—in a dog house—because that's where dogs belonged. My parents only let them inside for short, supervised periods, or until my mother came unglued because of dog hair or paw prints on her clean floors.

Now, for the first time in my adult life, I had my own dog. I could start fresh. The old dog covenant was gone, and I could create a new covenant with my chosen pooch.

I decided to cut up my back door to give Gracie free access to my house. This was a big deal to me for three reasons. First, I was breaking from old traditions. Second, I was defacing my home by cutting a hole in a perfectly good door. Third, it brought new meaning to the word many single men fear: *commitment*. Cutting that door meant I was accepting Gracie as a member of my family—long-term. This was no doggie sleepover or temporary dog-sitting assignment.

The door was an instant hit with Gracie. Before it existed, she had to ask if she happened to be inside and wanted out. She had to let me know with her body language: whining, scratching, yearning looks. And if she wanted to come in, she had to bark and scratch as well—and wait, perhaps for hours, if I wasn't home.

I thought I saw a big smile on her face the first few times Gracie went through her door—as though she'd discovered the secret to supernaturally passing through what was once solid wood. The door was a blessing to us both. And I made it for Gracie because, well, I loved that dog.

Like Gracie, I get a big smile on my face when I consider the "door" my Master made for me. He made that door because He loved me, because He didn't want to leave me at the mercy of demon coyotes and snakes and that roaring lion, the devil. So God provided a doorway for me into His holy and protective sanctuary—at a very high cost.

John 3:16 says, "God so loved the world that He gave His only begotten Son, that whoever believes in Him should not perish but have everlasting life" (NKJV). And in John 10:9, Jesus declares, "I am the door. If anyone enters by Me, he will be saved, and will go in and out and find pasture" (NKJV).

It's so appropriate and amazing that Jesus Christ calls Himself "the door."

The greatest gift I've ever received is my salvation. I don't dwell on it nearly enough. I'm sure that at first, like Gracie, I was thrilled to be allowed to come into my Master's sanctuary anytime I wanted. But these days, I sometimes take it for granted. I sometimes forget the cost of the door. God's love and Jesus' sacrifice were what gave me access to God's spiritual house, so I could become His child and find shelter and refuge in His presence.

Some time ago I was on a ferry crossing the English Channel. The waters were especially choppy. I have never known such seasickness in my life. The four-hour trip to land seemed an eternity. I had nowhere to escape. Motion sickness pills were useless, and sleep wouldn't come. I felt utterly ill until I laid myself down on a bench and began to pray. I recited Scripture and sang two Christian songs I had memorized. To make a long seasick story short, I walked through God's door and found shelter in the sanctuary of my Lord. I entered into "the peace of God, which surpasses all understanding" (Philippians 4:7 NKJV). I was in the presence of the same Jesus who had calmed the wind and sea for His fearful disciples.

When the ferry finally landed, I was so incredibly thankful—not just for dry land, but for God's door to peace *in the middle of the ocean, in the midst of the storm.* And through the years, I've found that no matter what kind of boat I'm trapped on, no matter if the storms are physical, emotional, or spiritual—the door to God's sanctuary is always open.

It makes me smile to think how Gracie loved her special door. I think God smiles when we love the door He gave us. After all He sacrificed, what a shame it would be if we didn't use it.

Enter into His gates with thanksgiving, and into His courts with praise (Psalm 100:4 NKJV).

Consider This

Was there a stormy time in your life when entering through God's door transformed your point of view? How did it change? What did you learn? How has it affected your walk with the Lord, and your readiness to go through the door should hard times hit again?

Part II

Obedience Training

Duck and Chocolate

Are You Keeping Something Back from God?

God will forgive me; it's His trade.

HEINRICH HEINE

Stuart loves to play games. Fetch is one of his favorites. He'll play fetch with any of his toys, but he likes Duck the best. Duck was once a soft, white, plush, stuffed animal—a gift to one of our children at Easter time. When Stuart got him, it didn't take long for Duck to lose anything we would call beautiful. Yet, the more ragged and chewed he became, the more Stuart loved him.

Stuart knew the names of all his toys and would bring them on command. One day, my husband Steve asked Stuart to bring Duck. Stuart raced off and returned with his tire instead.

"No, Stuart," Steve insisted. "Bring Duck."

Stuart went back to the special place where he keeps Duck, looked at him, and fetched his rubber bone.

Steve wasn't having any of it. "I said, bring Duck!"

Stuart brought Steve every toy he had *except* Duck. He knew exactly what Steve was asking for, but he refused to obey. "We won't play until you bring Duck," Steve told him. But Stuart kept on balking and offering other toys in Duck's place. This went on for the rest of the day and evening.

The next afternoon, Steve said, "Okay, Stuart, bring Duck." Stuart looked at him, rushed off, and returned with the requested toy. He dropped Duck at my husband's feet and then laid his head on Steve's shoe—his way of saying he's sorry. "Good boy, Stuart," Steve beamed. "Good boy." He gave Stuart a hug and they began to play Stuart's favorite game once more.

Stuart loves Steve and is normally faithful and obedient to him. Why he chose to behave in this fashion is beyond us. Was this a game to him also? Whatever the cause, from time to time Stuart still refuses to bring Duck, and we don't know the reason.

What we do know is how Stuart's disobedience affects his relationship with Steve. It strains the connection between them. They don't enjoy each other as much. But when Stuart repents, Steve gladly forgives, and their connection is restored with joy.

This has made me think about my connection with my Master.

I love my Lord, and He loves me. I love feeling close to Him, talking to Him, and experiencing His guidance. But just like Stuart, I sometimes disobey. I sometimes balk at bringing Him a certain special something in my life. I bring Him everything else *but* that. I lay my marriage at His feet. I give Him my children, my work, my home, my friends. And He is glad, but He wants more. His still small voice says, "Connie, bring chocolate."

As I'm writing this, I want to leave my desk, grab a candy bar from the kitchen, plop in front of the TV, and enjoy it. Why is this wrong? Because I'm overweight and diabetic. It's for my good that my Master has asked me to lay my food choices at His feet. But I have trouble giving over my will in this area of my life. I want to keep chocolate in my special place. I want to hold it back, just like Stuart did with Duck.

It's a constant struggle. When I manage to bring chocolate, I feel happy and complete. My Master is pleased. Our connection is strong. But it doesn't take much for me to stumble and disobey again.

As a teacher, I feel extra pressure when an Open House is coming up. This is when parents visit their children's classrooms, see their work, and talk with their teachers. I recall a particular day when my students and I had been preparing for one of these. In addition to our normal class work, we had done some special projects. We had made a rocket ship where a student could sit and read. We had made flight suits for each student with special patches all over. We had written a book about our class flying into space. Each of these projects had left a huge mess of paper, markers, scissors, and glue. Even though I had the students clean up before they left, I still had some mop-up to do, not to mention getting ready for the next day.

When I'd finally said my last goodbye and my room was empty of people, I sank down in my chair, raised my arms, and shouted, "Chocolate!" Earlier that same day, I had given my food to God. But at this moment, I didn't care about being obedient. I didn't care if what I was doing was healthy. I was convinced that the only way I could finish my work, go home and make dinner, be kind to my family, go to choir practice, and gear up for another busy day tomorrow was to satisfy my craving for chocolate.

I reached in a drawer where I had a hefty stash of candy. I don't think one or two small pieces would have hurt me. But I knew I wouldn't stop there, and I didn't. I ate several pieces.

I got through the rest of my work and my day. I did everything I was supposed to. Everything but check my blood sugar, that is. I didn't have to. I knew it was high. My body felt lousy, and so did my spirit. Before I went to sleep, I came to the Father in prayer and begged His forgiveness once more. And He hugged me and restored our connection—just as Steve did with Stuart.

God doesn't forget about me when I'm disobedient, any more than Steve forgets about Stuart. But it hurts our connection, and I don't want that to happen. I don't want a break in our closeness. I don't want to grieve Him. And so, no matter what else I have brought, I will try to obey when He says in His still, small voice, "Connie, bring chocolate."

Samuel replied: "Does the LORD delight in burnt offerings and sacrifices as much as in obeying the voice of the LORD? To obey is better than sacrifice, and to heed is better than the fat of rams" (1 Samuel 15:22).

Consider This

Is there something God has asked you to bring Him that you are holding back? What makes it hard to put this at His feet? What would help you obey and restore the connection between you?

The Dog Who Washed Feet

We Are Called to Be Servants

For it is in giving that we receive....

<small>SAINT FRANCIS OF ASSISI</small>

I used to joke that Morgan is a Christian dog because he washes feet. If mine are bare, he goes to work. Sometimes he even cleans between the toes. Of course, his reason for doing so is not remotely connected to anything that we read in the Bible. He's probably just licking salt off my skin. He washes my chin and fingers too. But this innocent doggie practice got me thinking about biblical foot washing and its implications for my life.

In Bible times people walked long distances in sandals. Their feet were dusty and dirty when they reached their destination. In poorer households, hospitable hosts brought water so their guests could wash their own feet. In wealthy homes, the lowliest servants did the foot washing. It showed special humility or love if the master (or mistress) of the home performed this service for a guest.

At the Last Supper, Jesus washed His disciples' feet. There are multiple meanings in this, but surely one is servanthood. Christ was setting an example to encourage His followers to love and humbly serve each other.

Some years ago I attended a Passover seder that combined traditional elements of the Jewish seder with a foot washing ceremony. We passed a basin and towel around and bathed each others' feet. I had brought my mother, and I was privileged to wash hers. That memory is deeply meaningful because I have struggled with having a servant's heart toward Mom, and God has worked to change that.

I recall a trip Mom and I took overseas some years ago. She had paid my way. She desired my companionship and help. She'd had some problems with her eyes, and while she could still get around, she didn't see as clearly as she once had. In strange surroundings, she felt a bit disoriented. She wanted me to stay close, but I like my space, and I started feeling somewhat claustrophobic.

I have to confess, I had more of a rebel's than a servant's heart. I was grumpy and kept trying to slip off by myself. Mom understood and let me go, but I'm sure at times it hurt her. I didn't act as Jesus would have, and I'm ashamed of it now.

But God has been at work in me, convicting me of my selfishness and planting a desire in my heart to be more like Christ. And He has given me new chances to love and serve my mother. One tiny recent example comes to mind.

Mom and I both love orchids. She even has a small greenhouse on her property. Periodically, there are orchid shows in the city where she lives. Once a year, a special orchid sale is held. She and I both used to attend these sales. But she is 89 now and has had some health challenges, so I go for both of us.

God has given me increasing joy in being Mom's personal shopper, finding just the plants I think she'll like. I've become less concerned about getting the ones I want and more eager to brighten her life.

This last time, after I brought the plants home, Mom wanted to take me on a tour of her garden. She isn't as steady as she once was, and she needs someone to hold on to when she does this. I was able to serve her by being her walking stick, or, as she put it, her mobile handrail. For probably an hour, she tugged me hither and yon as she inspected various plants and shared their beauty with her only daughter.

Some days after the sale, Mom called to thank me. She had put the orchids all over her house. Some were scented. Her home was filled with fragrance and color. Hearing her pleasure flooded me with joy. I received far more than I gave with my tiny act of service. God multiplied the blessing.

I wonder if that's because true servanthood is an expression of love. I see this in how Morgan responds to me. He does his doggie best to please and obey me…most of the time. He tries to comfort me when I'm down. He lets me hold him close beneath the covers on a cold winter's night so his warm little body can be my living heater. I sense his love in these small doggie gestures, and it conquers my heart.

Christ's own disciples didn't understand the power of servanthood. They were more concerned about who would be greatest in His kingdom. But He told them to focus on serving instead. In Matthew 20:26-28, He urged, "Whoever wants to become great among you must be your servant, and whoever wants to be first must be your slave—just as the Son of Man did not come to be served, but to serve, and to give his life as a ransom for many."

Jesus served and overcame the world. If we serve in love as He did, we can be "more than conquerors" in Him (Romans 8:37).

Your attitude should be the same as that of Christ Jesus: Who, being in very nature God, did

not consider equality with God something to be grasped, but made himself nothing, taking the very nature of a servant, being made in human likeness (Philippians 2:5-7).

Consider This

How might you be more of a servant to your loved ones? Your friends? Your coworkers? Your local church body? Your community?

Train Up a Dog
God's Discipline May Prevent Greater Pain

Do not consider painful
what is good for you.

EURIPEDES

Early in our relationship, I went out to get the mail and Gracie rushed ahead of me, bounding toward the street. I yelled at her to stop, but she was too excited about being outside to listen to me. As she raced across the asphalt, I saw a car approaching on a collision course with my new dog. Before I could call out, the car screeched to a stop, barely avoiding smacking Gracie into doggie heaven.

Relieved, I grabbed her collar and pulled her to safety. I thanked God she was okay, but I was angry that she had almost gotten herself killed. I grabbed a newspaper, rolled it up, and led Gracie back to the end of my driveway. I told her she was not to step into the street without my permission. I looked her in the eyes when I said this and believed she understood me. Then, to bring the point home, I held her nose to the boundary line and sternly told her, "No! Never cross this line unless I'm with you!" I then proceeded to give her a few whacks with the rolled-up newspaper. I'd never had my own dog before, so I didn't know if spanking was politically correct—but it's what I instinctively did.

There might have been a better way to get my point across, but Gracie understood completely. She never violated that boundary line again as long as she lived. No matter how excited she was about going for her walk, she always waited at the end of the driveway until I led her forth.

I've mused on how God has often had to deal with me in a similar way. Like Gracie, I've rushed into things without checking with my Master. I've put myself in danger. Occasionally, I've fallen and hurt myself. But God has always been there to lift me up, take me back to safety—and, when warranted, administer a spiritual spanking with a rolled-up newspaper of His own design for my future benefit and well-being. It made my lesson visceral as well as verbal and certainly drove the point home.

While there are more dramatic examples of being spanked and corrected, the one that comes to mind is a tiny but important incident.

Once in a while I've gotten uncanceled postage stamps in the mail; stamps stuck on letters and packages that escaped being inked on in the back rooms of post offices. For most of my life, finding one of these was like winning a micro-mini lottery. I would cut out the stamp, soak it off, and reuse it. I would feel good about my luck and even think I was doing something positive in a "recycling" sense. Like Gracie rushing down the driveway and into the street, I was just following my natural instincts and had never stopped to think there was anything wrong with what I was doing.

Then one day I received a 55-cent stamp that was unblemished. I proceeded to do what I had always done. Suddenly, a Scripture I had memorized long ago came into my mind. It was Philippians 4:19: "My God will meet all your needs according to his glorious riches in Christ Jesus."

It was like a tug on my spiritual choke chain, a stern "No!" command to my heart, a whack on my spiritual bottom with a rolled-up newspaper. I understood completely that God didn't want me to reuse that postage stamp. I felt as much conviction from my Master as I'd had when I warned Gracie not to rush into the street.

My brain went into an internal dialogue with my Creator.

God: "Kris, why are you reusing that stamp?"

Me: "Because as a freelance writer, I've sometimes worked for years without earning a penny, so I'm trained to take advantage of any and every rebate."

God: "Why?"

And then, I found myself standing in the middle of the street with the answer speeding toward me like a 1966 Cadillac: "Because I don't really believe that You will meet all my needs according to Your glorious riches in Christ Jesus."

The Caddy screeched to a stop, the big chrome bumper just grazing my shin.

God pulled me gently back to the safety of His driveway and convicted my heart. I think spiritual conviction is akin to God taking a rolled-up newspaper to our hindquarters. And yes, it hurt me, just like it hurt Gracie, but I knew it was for my best.

God set a boundary for me that day. He drew a line He didn't want me to cross. He didn't want me to put other suppliers of my needs before Him. He didn't want me to cheat over a 55-cent postage stamp when as His child I have access to His promise that *all* my needs will be met according to His *glorious riches* in Christ.

I've received other uncanceled stamps in the mail over the years. It takes discipline to toss them in the trash, but I do it because God knows what's best for me. I feel I will enter into a fuller, more abundant life because of this simple correction by my Master. I am learning to choose God's "glorious best" by faith instead of settling for the "55-cent good things" I perceive by sight.

Because Gracie obeyed me, she was spared an untimely death from being hit by a car. She led a full and abundant life as my precious dog, and she passed away of natural causes. I thank God that

He disciplines me so I, too, can live out the full and abundant life He has planned for me.

Our fathers disciplined us for a little while as they thought best; but God disciplines us for our good, that we may share in his holiness. No discipline seems pleasant at the time, but painful. Later on, however, it produces a harvest of righteousness and peace for those who have been trained by it (Hebrews 12:10-11).

Consider This

What are some ways God has disciplined you? How did you first react to His correction? How do you see it now, in hindsight? What harvest have you reaped from His training?

Morgan, the Great Escape Dog

God's Boundaries Are for Our Good

Whoever digs a pit may fall into it; whoever breaks through a wall may be bitten by a snake.

ECCLESIASTES 10:8

Perhaps you have heard of a famed escape artist known as the Great Houdini. My dog Morgan was the Great Houdini of canines. He could climb. He could jump. He could wedge his small body through holes I never knew existed. Just when I thought I had gated him in at last, he found a new way out.

When Morgan came to live with me, my hilly yard was bounded north and south by wire fencing draped with ivy. Wooden fencing stretched across the back, and wrought iron gating and the house itself secured the yard's front border. Biscuit, my older dog, had been easily confined by these barriers.

Morgan quickly proved he could go where Biscuit never thought to tread.

I've written elsewhere about how Morgan's first foray from the yard was through a separation in the south-side fence. This was quickly corrected, but it didn't stop him for long. He turned his efforts to the north side of the yard, where large eucalyptus trees stood along the wire boundary like sentinels.

Did I say sentinels? For Morgan, they were launching pads.

The trees had low, elevated hollows where the trunks split off into limbs. Morgan climbed to these platforms and then scrambled onto the fence. From there he pulled himself up and over into the next yard.

I loved to let the dogs romp while I swam in my backyard pool. These were some of Morgan's favorite times to escape. While swimming laps I would call the dogs to check on them. He'd be gone, and then I'd have to race dripping wet out the gate to retrieve him.

Determined to thwart him, I got the gardeners to stuff the tree hollows with plants, hoping that would keep Morgan from getting a foothold. It worked. He was stymied.

But not for long!

The little scamp turned his attention to the south-side fence once more. He found gap after gap in the aging wire. I'd no sooner get one hole plugged than he'd slip through another. Fortunately, the adjoining yard was fenced. But finally he got through my neighbors' south fence and into a third yard with no gating. I gave up my futile patching efforts and bit the financial bullet. I had a whole new south-side fence installed just in front of the existing one. Morgan was contained at last.

Of course, he hadn't ignored his boundaries to be naughty or because he wanted to run away from me. He did it to chase birds and squirrels. He's a hunter. He thought he saw something good beyond the fence. To him, that boundary stood in the way of his pleasure. He didn't know it was for his benefit. He didn't realize he could be hurt or killed if he crossed it.

I've not always realized this with boundaries either.

Beginning in fourth grade, I struggled with weight. By high school, I had a real problem. My parents tried to curb my eating, but I resisted. I felt I had to be ready to diet or it wouldn't work. Midway through my junior year, I was. I wanted to be svelte and popular. I wanted a new me.

I took things too far.

By that summer, I had dropped my 5′2″ frame from 135 pounds to a low of 98. I had also developed an eating disorder. I was starving, then bingeing, and I was obsessive about my weight. I was also exercising compulsively.

I don't recall the specifics. I'm sure my parents tried various things to contain the situation, but they weren't working. They knew they had to make a boundary stick, and fast. If my anorexia went unchecked, it could lead to serious or even fatal health problems. Finally, my father erected one last desperate emotional fence. He gave me a choice. I could keep my weight at a healthy level with his help, or he would pull me out of school to get treatment.

A part of me realized I was in trouble, but I was chasing birds and squirrels. I wanted to be thinner. I felt I had a right to my own identity, and this was my way to get it. I was terribly resentful. But, like the final fence I would later erect for Morgan, I knew my father's boundary was firm. I saw no way around it. And, truth be told, I wanted help in keeping my weight off. In the end, I agreed.

Dad's boundary worked. And all these years later, I realize he saved me from untold harm. He knew better than I, and his fence was a sign of his love.

God knows better too. Our heavenly Father sets fences around us to save us from harm and death. Those fences are His Spirit and His Word. Though we long to chase the birds and squirrels of our fleshly desires, He sees the danger. We don't always understand His boundaries, and at times we resent them, but they are for our good and are a sign of His love.

Morgan doesn't escape anymore. I have less and less desire to wander too. I'd rather stay safe in my Master's yard, basking in His love, just as Morgan basks in mine.

In that day this song will be sung in the land of Judah: We have a strong city; God makes salvation its walls and ramparts (Isaiah 26:1).

Consider This

Can you think of a time in your life when God's fences saved you from danger? Did you recognize your peril at the time? What did you learn, and how has it influenced your life?

Seeing Eye Master
We Need God to Guide Us

Lead, kindly Light, amid the encircling gloom;
Lead thou me on!
The night is dark, and I am far from home;
Lead thou me on!
Keep thou my feet: I do not ask to see
The distant scene; one step enough for me.

JOHN HENRY CARDINAL NEWMAN

Max, our Boston terrier, was in our family for many years. He grew old as the children grew up. When his vision failed, he needed a Seeing Eye person. We tried to be that for him.

Though we lived on a country road, it was maintained for use by emergency vehicles, and cars often sped past our home. We had to watch Max closely, and he had to listen for us. Once I looked up from weeding and spied him wandering near the road just as a huge truck rumbled toward him. Max didn't see it. I yelled his name. He stopped in his tracks and turned, heading toward me and away from harm.

One morning as I watched Max from our den window, I saw him trying to navigate the yard without our voices to guide him.

He carefully made his way down the sidewalk, but as he stepped onto the driveway he smacked into my car. If one of the family had been outside, we would have been able to lead him. "No, Max, come this way. Over here, Max. Watch out, Max. (Bump!) Oh, Max!" He learned to adjust his path by our voices…at least, most of the time.

Which reminds me of how I, too, have been guided by my Seeing Eye Master.

Steve and I married young. We were 19 and 20 years old. Soon after, we moved from our hometown of Bakersfield, California, to Whittier. Steve attended college and I supported us with a tiny salary by working in a bank. But our sights were set on the mission field. I had felt the call years earlier, following a missions trip to Japan. Now Steve took a Japanese language course along with his college studies. As our certainty deepened, we applied to our church's mission board.

Then one day, as we were taking a walk and discussing our future, we stopped and prayed for guidance, just as we had done so many times before. We felt our Master nudging our hearts. To our surprise, God seemed to be prompting us to move back to our hometown. We couldn't see why. Confused, we prayed for confirmation.

We were shocked and a little disappointed when a letter came from the mission board, telling us that to be accepted, one of us must have a college degree. Neither of us did. We prayed some more. Again God's still small voice whispered to our hearts, "Go home."

We packed up our slightly used wedding gifts and moved back to Bakersfield. Steve began working for his father on the family farm. Shortly after, Steve's mom was diagnosed with cancer. Her only son was a great comfort to her during her illness.

A few months later, early in the morning, as Steve and I were making breakfast in our little farm home, we received a call that my dad had suffered a heart attack and had gone home to be with his

Savior. God had seen what we could not…that our families would need us…and He had led us back to them.

We guided Max because we loved him; he was part of our family. Much more, God guides us because He loves us and we belong to Him.

Whether you turn to the right or to the left, your ears will hear a voice behind you, saying, "This is the way; walk in it" (Isaiah 30:21).

Consider This

What are some of the ways God uses to speak to and guide His children? How has He used them to guide you in your life? What can you do to become more sensitive to His still small voice?

A Woof of Warning
Hear and Heed God's Voice

Forewarned is forearmed.

PROVERB

In our new home, we have a brand-new, modern security system. I'm sure it's wonderful—but we're not used to it. In the past, our alarm system has always been our dogs.

Huxley made an especially good warning system. He even had different barks for different people and vehicles. We had a friend who drove a white pickup. When he came to see us, he always brought his dog. Huxley wasn't happy when that dog came into the yard and woofed in a hostile, protective way whenever the pickup approached. But Huxley always barked a friendly hello when the UPS truck pulled up to our home. He liked the driver, who greeted him warmly and sometimes brought him treats.

Because of Huxley, we felt secure. We came to know his various barks. We were confident that he would warn us if there was a problem. One night there was, and he tried...but we didn't listen.

It was very late, and we were all asleep. Huxley started woofing, and he wouldn't quit. It sounded like the bark he used to signal strangers, but even more intense. Those of us who heard him knew we should get up, get dressed, and check things out. But we gave in to our fatigue and stayed under the covers, wishing he would fall silent so we could get back to sleep.

The next morning, Steve went out to the big tin shed he uses as a workshop and discovered that we'd been robbed. The shed contained many expensive tools and machinery essential for farming. The thieves had stolen a number of tools, and they had also taken an old motorcycle our son had bought to restore. All this had happened while we lay in bed, ignoring our faithful dog's warning.

Our heavenly Father also wants to protect us from impending danger. He uses His Word, His Spirit, His children, and our circumstances to warn us. But we don't always heed Him either…as I haven't with exercise.

In 1 Corinthians 6:19-20, Paul writes, "Do you not know that your body is a temple of the Holy Spirit, who is in you, whom you have received from God? You are not your own; you were bought at a price. Therefore honor God with your body."

In the context of the passage, Paul is warning believers against sexual sin. But I think these verses have a broader meaning. Our bodies are a gift from God, and He wants us to take good care of them. For me, this means getting more exercise. I know God wants me to do it. His Spirit has convicted my heart. But I've been ignoring His warning. It's not just that I'm lazy; I have arthritis, and exercising can be painful. But because I don't do it, my body is getting weaker.

Recently, two dear friends of mine tried to help. They suggested that we ride bikes together. We all needed to lose weight, and they thought this would be great for me. My husband bought me a wonderful new bicycle for my birthday in March. But then I got sick. One of my friends did too. Life got in the way. It's now August, and we haven't ridden together yet.

Meanwhile, Steve and I and our daughter Karen moved to a new home. Being out of shape made it that much harder on me. Had I started exercising, the physical work of the move might have seemed less strenuous, my health would have been better, and I would know that I had been obedient to my Lord.

At times, it seems troublesome to heed God's warnings. We'd much rather stay in bed and hope the barking stops. But if we do, we may discover that things, such as good health, have been stolen from us. The Lord always warns us for our good, to spare us greater grief. So listen for His voice, and heed it while you can.

Show us your unfailing love, O LORD, and grant us your salvation. I will listen to what God the LORD will say; he promises peace to his people (Psalm 85:7-8).

Consider This

Can you think of a time when you ignored a warning and it caused you grief? Why did you ignore it? What did it cost you? Did it impact loved ones also? If so, how?

Is there a warning in your life you need to heed right now? How can you do so?

God's Pop Quizzes

Do You Pass Life's Small Tests?

Practice makes perfect.

PROVERB

When I was a kid, my teachers used to give us pop quizzes—mini tests sprung on us to see how well we knew our lessons.

I sometimes give Biscuit and Morgan pop quizzes to see how well they know their commands.

One recent quiz happened at the back door as my hungry-faced pooches prepared to blast past me to their food bowls to inhale their morning kibble. Biscuit bounced at the screen, impatient as always.

"Sit. Stay."

The dogs obeyed, poised to launch through the door that would now surely open for them. Instead, I walked away. I wanted to see if they'd hold still till I told them they could move. It took a few tries till both dogs remained in place for a long enough time that I felt they had passed, and then I let them in.

I throw other quizzes at them too. I make them sit in front of their food until I release them to eat. Up in my office, I ask them to "down" or "high-five" or "roll" when I'm on a writing break. Some commands I've taught them are just frivolous fun, but I know others could be crucial if a serious test came along. If my dogs got loose by accident and beelined toward danger, the "come" command could call them back and save their little necks.

In the same way, my Master gives me pop quizzes on His commands so I'll be prepared for the larger tests of life. One memorable quiz involved the command "Give thanks in all circumstances" (1 Thessalonians 5:18).

It came on the morning of my annual physical exam. I awoke to discover we'd had a power outage. As I prepared for my appointment and got the animals fed and watered, I kept hoping the juice would come back on. My car was captured in the garage, and I wasn't sure I remembered how to release the door and lift it manually.

The clock ticked down to appointment time. The power stayed off. I realized it was time to do battle with the door. I got it released just fine…but I couldn't raise it to save my life. It was stuck…and so was I. Teeth grinding, blood pressure rising, frustration boiling over, I dashed upstairs and phoned a friend who lived nearby. She couldn't take me.

By now I was nearly beside myself. I was primed for that appointment. I had done a little "prep" for it that I didn't care to repeat. I thought of calling a taxi, but I seldom take them, and I feared the wait for one might be too long. The doctor's office was less than a ten-minute drive from home. My stress-muddled brain seized the only solution it saw. I would walk.

I phoned the doctor's office from my cell phone as I started down the street. They said not to worry…they'd fit me in when I got there. Then I dealt with the pop quiz I knew God was giving me. "Lord, I hate this. I'm angry. I don't want to thank You, but Your Word says to give thanks in all things. So thank You for the power outage. Thank You for the stuck door." Then I added a little something extra. My appointment had been for 9:15. I prayed I could get to the doctor by 9:45.

Yeah, right!

I'd badly underestimated the time it would take me to hoof it. As my watch ticked past 9:30, I knew there was no way I was going to make it on foot. The weather matched my mood...overcast and slightly chilly. And then a cab appeared behind me. It caught up and pulled over. The driver leaned out and asked if I needed a ride.

Bells clanged. Lights flashed. I felt as though God had dropped a chariot from heaven. Minutes later, I was at the doctor's office—at the time I'd prayed for. By now I was spilling over with joy, proclaiming God's providence to all who'd listen. We got the exam done. Later, the walk home took almost an hour. (What was I thinking!)

As I reflect on it, all life's frustrations are really pop quizzes, aren't they? Traffic jams, lines at the grocery store, the burst pipe or overflowing toilet, the error on a bill that takes hours to straighten out—all are mini tests to prep us for the larger challenges of life. If I can't thank God for a power outage, what will I do if I get cancer, or a loved one dies, or my home is badly damaged in a fire? If I don't learn patience in the small annoyances, how will I have patience and endurance when a big trial hits?

I am grateful that God takes time to prepare me, as my teachers did, and as I do with my dogs. Praise God for His training, His Word, His commands.

Praise God for pop quizzes!

Have nothing to do with godless myths and old wives' tales; rather, train yourself to be godly. For physical training is of some value, but godliness has value for all things, holding promise for both

the present life and the life to come (1 Timothy 4:7-8).

Consider This

What are some of the more memorable pop quizzes God has given you? Did you pass or fail? What did you learn? How have they prepared you for larger tests you've faced?

Who's Afraid of the Big Bad Dog?

Fear God, Not Man

Make God thy Friend, and then it's
no matter who is thy Enemy.

Thomas Fuller

Huxley was a great big wonderful mixed-breed farm dog. He loved to go out in the fields and play in the mud. He loved frolicking in the front yard with the family. But his favorite place to be was our backyard. This was where he did most of his watchdog work. This was where he ate and slept. This was his kingdom, and he was the king. Except for our little Boston terrier, Max, no other animals were allowed to intrude on his territory.

Not that the cats didn't try.

We've had many cats in our years on the farm. We've tried to name them all. We've named them after presidents: George, Abe, and Ron. We've named them after clothes labels: Reebok, Armani, Izod, and Nike. We've given them names that rhyme: Esther, Wester, Chester, and Lester. And one time, our sweet mama cat had a litter of kittens on our roof. So we named them Atticus, Roofus, and Wally. (Wall-y, get it?)

These cats all had something in common. They all crept into Huxley's world. When they ventured into his life, he was quick to notice. He'd jump up from his resting place and give chase as they raced across the backyard and into the almond orchard. Sometimes he even climbed up a tree after them.

Huxley loved chasing cats because he knew they hated it. He knew they'd run from him. He knew they were all afraid of the big bad dog. But there was one tiny kitten, Wally, who did not succumb to Huxley's torment.

Wally got his name because he fell from the roof down into the wall of our house. Our son, John, rescued him with a towel and fishing line. He tied the towel to the line and lowered it down to the stranded cat. When Wally grabbed on, John reeled him back up.

Wally was a runt. He was one of the smallest kittens we've ever had, but he didn't seem aware of how tiny he was. Or maybe he just didn't believe Huxley was the big bad enemy. Whatever the cause, Wally chose to approach instead of run.

The first time we saw Wally in the backyard, we all ran to save him. Tiny Wally was walking along the backyard fence. Huxley lay by his food dish, watching. Wally marched right over and lowered his head into the bowl, and then he looked up at its owner. Huxley eyed the intruder in apparent disbelief. Didn't this little pest know what he had done to others for a lesser offense? Huxley could have swallowed Wally in one bite. This kitten should have been terrified.

But Wally wasn't...and Huxley must have sensed it. He must have sensed that his scare tactics wouldn't work on this cat. They soon became friends. Huxley let Wally share his food. Wally climbed up on Huxley and took naps on the big dog's back. The two remained pals till the day Wally died.

This made me think of a time when I felt small, like Wally, and encountered someone who seemed big and imposing, like Huxley. I had ventured into his kingdom...Hollywood. I was interested in acting and had gone with some friends to hear a speaker at Hollywood Presbyterian Church.

Michael was a literary agent. He spoke more about writing and producing than acting. I looked at his polished appearance, his beautiful silk suit and shiny shoes, and I thought, *This man lives in a different world. Why am I here?* But as I continued to listen, I felt my heavenly Father prompting me to pray for him.

After the meeting, I wrote my email address on a piece of paper. When I walked up to Michael, there were many people around him. I thought I'd have no chance to talk to him, but it seemed God kept pushing me closer. Suddenly, he looked at me. I said, "Michael, I know I'm here because I'm supposed to pray for you."

He thanked me and gave me his email address, asking that I wait to contact him. He'd be too busy to respond right then, but would I get back to him in a few weeks?

Though I thought that would be the end of it, I did as he asked. I emailed and told him I'd been praying for him. He answered, thanking me and sharing some prayer requests. He told me others had contacted him (he'd given his email address to several that night), but he felt led of God to respond to me. We began a friendship that continues to this day. We've become prayer warriors for one another, sharing prayer concerns and Scripture. When I sent him some of my stories, he encouraged me to write more. Because of the writing, and my passion to pray for Hollywood, he suggested I join a group of Christians in the entertainment industry who gather once a month for worship and intercession.

I don't know for sure how Wally felt the first time he marched up to Huxley, but I know how I felt when I walked up to Michael that first night. I felt small and nervous. However, I told myself, "God made him, God made me, and God is in control." Because I obeyed God despite my fear and reached out as He had told me to, I made a new friend and a new world opened up.

I have found that facing fear is the best way to fight it. Sometimes the worst enemy is the fear itself. But victory comes when I seek the Lord and ask Him to cover me and guard me and guide me through. Michael is a huge blessing in my life, just as Huxley was in Wally's, because neither of us let fear stand in the way of friendship.

Fear of man will prove to be a snare, but whoever trusts in the LORD is kept safe (Proverbs 29:25).

Consider This

Are there people in your life who seem big and imposing, like Huxley? Do you fear them? What about them scares you? If God asked you to reach out to them, would you be willing? Why, or why not?

Reach for the Master
God Is Our Refuge

The eternal God is your refuge, and
underneath are the everlasting arms.

DEUTERONOMY 33:27

Some weeks ago, I hauled my two dogs and four cats in for checkups and shots. Their young female vet is sensitive and gentle, but Morgan still wasn't too sure about things. As she started to take him, he turned away and reached for his mommy—me!

When it comes to people, Morgan's much more of a scaredy-dog than Biscuit. In the vet's waiting room, he's the one who must be on my lap. He feels safer there, while Biscuit's content to curl up near my feet or even strain on her leash toward a friendly looking stranger.

Morgan's also more hesitant when new people come to the house. If I'm there, he'll warm up and make friends. But if I leave him alone with the newcomer, even briefly, he is apt to become afraid and bark anxiously till I return.

Morgan was a rescue, and I've guessed there was some kind of trauma in his past. But he knows I'm his master and I love him, and he trusts me. Whatever his fears, if I'm there, he feels safer. I am Morgan's refuge.

God is my refuge!

I've needed one. According to family lore, I was practically born scared. Mom says the doctor pronounced me a worrier at birth. Apparently there was something about my behavior, even as a newborn, that made him think I'd be a frequent fretter. He wasn't wrong. Even as a small child, I cringed at turning another year older—because it brought me another year closer to death. I was also uptight about tests, rejection, new challenges I feared I might fail…the list goes on and on. Fear was a big part of my life.

For the last four decades, God has been a big part of my life as well. This has not made all my fears go away, but I have learned to deal with them differently. I have learned to reach for Him when I'm scared and draw strength from His presence, even if I'm terrified of the situation at hand.

One such "reach for God" time involved an organization I belonged to. I was on the steering committee this particular year. Though we were all Christians, there had been some dissension, and I looked forward with some trepidation to our annual business meeting.

That trepidation turned to dread when the person slated to lead the meeting had to leave town on business. She asked me to take her place if she couldn't get back. I tried to demur. I feared I'd flub it. I feared I'd make matters worse, and disgrace and embarrass myself in the bargain. I didn't even know the needed parliamentary procedure. Surely there had to be someone better for the task!

But God wouldn't let me off the hook. He made it clear He wanted me to do this. Still shaking inside, I said yes and reached for Him. I chose to believe He'd provide what I needed for what He had called me to. And in the days that followed, He did.

Other members with experience and skills I lacked called to offer their help and support. God gave me people to pray with personally. The day of the meeting, we prayed and worshipped first.

God guided us, and though differences were aired, we ended in détente.

The way I've sought refuge in God has changed as I've matured in Him. I used to want Him to remove what was scaring me. I wanted Him to be my great big Problem Solver in the sky. Now I realize at times it's His will for me to go through a trial. When this happens, I must reach for His strength, His comfort, and His presence to sustain me.

I had to do this a few months ago, when my mom almost died. She had a severe staph infection and was put on potent antibiotics. Perhaps the drugs made her restless. In any case, she was hardly sleeping. At times, her thinking seemed confused...probably from sleep deprivation. But Mom had always been in charge and insisted on remaining so. I wasn't ready for her to die. I didn't know what to do. I felt as though I were scrabbling for footing on a ship spinning out of control.

I reached for my Master—for His strength and His presence, whatever the outcome of this storm. I reached for His people... Christian friends who offered prayer and counsel. And I reached for His Word...including a Scripture a friend shared about the battle belonging to God—though I wasn't sure what that meant in my situation.

What it turned out to mean was that God took care of what I couldn't manage. Mom improved, her mental sharpness was restored, and I learned a whole new lesson in faith.

In the end, it's by faith that I reach for my Master. Unlike Morgan, who can see and touch me, I can't see and touch my Lord. I can't always feel His presence, either. But I know what He's done for me in the past. And I know what He says in His Word. He says He's my rock, my fortress, my strong tower.

I don't have to fear even my fears when I have a God like that.

Even though I walk through the valley of the shadow of death, I will fear no evil, for you are with me; your rod and your staff, they comfort me (Psalm 23:4).

Consider This

What are the things you fear most in life? Why are they so scary to you? When these fears come up, do you reach for your Master? How do you do that? How does He sustain you? How might He use you to help sustain others?

A Bucket of Trust
God Will Meet Your Needs

All I have seen teaches me to trust
the Creator for all I have not seen.

RALPH WALDO EMERSON

Mealtime was the highlight of Gracie's day. The dog loved to eat. When I went out to feed her each morning, she became so excited her tail wagged her whole body. But her look of delirious joy wasn't based on the level of dry food stored in our five-gallon plastic bucket. Gracie had no idea that sometimes it was filled to the brim, while other times it was nearly empty—just a day's supply left. I never caught her, in a secret moment, cleverly using her paws to lift the lid and peek inside. Nor would she have dreamed of writing "dog food" on our shopping list…even if she could.

Gracie didn't look to the bucket or the store for her needs…she looked to me, her master.

It's dawned on me that I, too, have a Master who cares for me. He has even promised, in writing, to supply *all* my needs "according to his glorious riches in Christ Jesus" (Philippians 4:19). And yet, how often have I fixed my eyes on the provision, rather than the Provider?

When my son was born, my wife and I decided she should quit her teaching job and stay home with him for his first two years of life. During those two years, my income as a writer dried up like a stream in summer. We lived on our savings and my part-time teaching salary. It was barely enough to cover the bills. I knew God's many promises to provide for those He loves. But every month when I got my credit union statement showing how little was in our "plastic bucket," I panicked, worried, and wondered. Should I get a normal job? Should my wife go back to work earlier than we'd planned? I lost countless anxious hours staring down at the bucket…hours God meant for peace if I'd only gazed up at the bucket-Filler instead.

In hindsight, I can see all the gifts and favors God bestowed. I can see how He met all our needs during those years. And now that our income has improved and there's more in our bucket again, I realize my worries were a waste of perfectly good time. My beloved Master was watching out for us all along, but I didn't fully trust Him.

In all the years I had Gracie, I never let her starve. If anything, I fed her a little too well. Some folks even commented on her full-figured body. She wasn't anxious about her provision because she knew her master loved her and would take care of her. She trusted me with all her heart.

How much more will our Father in heaven care for us—if we'll only trust in Him the same way.

Then Jesus said to his disciples: "Therefore I tell you, do not worry about your life, what you will eat; or about your body, what you will wear.

Life is more than food, and the body more than clothes. Consider the ravens: They do not sow or reap, they have no storeroom or barn; yet God feeds them. And how much more valuable you are than birds!" (Luke 12:22-24).

Consider This

How much time do you spend staring at your bucket? How much time do you spend focusing on your bucket-Filler? Do these numbers need to be reversed?

Who Moved My Yard?
Let God Expand Your Territory

Change is not made without inconve-
nience, even from worse to better.

RICHARD HOOKER

When Stuart was a little puppy, he spent plenty of time with us in our home, but we also gave him his own space outside. His little fenced yard had bushes and grass and a beautiful view of the farm. It met all his needs, but it was quite small. The big backyard was where Huxley, our old mixed-breed farm dog, lived. Huxley and Stuart could see each other. They played together at times. But we thought it was best to give them their own separate spots until they got to know each other better.

When Huxley died, Stuart gained ownership of our big back-yard. It was probably six times larger than his small one had been. It had great places to run and play. Yet, when he'd run loose on the farm for a while and it came time to relax, Stuart kept heading back to his small, familiar yard to do so.

Stuart also resisted change in the house. We'd kept his food and water in a special place. We thought of another spot that would be more convenient for him. But when we moved his dishes, Stuart promptly dragged them back.

Although we were offering Stuart bigger and better things, things we knew would improve his life, he tried to retreat to the old and familiar. But because we loved him, we persisted. We kept on putting him in the big yard. We kept on moving his dishes. Finally, he accepted the changes, and they blessed him.

I have a copy of the Jabez prayer posted on my computer:

> Jabez cried out to the God of Israel, "Oh, that you would bless me and enlarge my territory! Let your hand be with me, and keep me from harm so that I will be free from pain." And God granted his request (1 Chronicles 4:10).

It's there to remind me that I want God to expand my territory. Yet when He does, I often complain. Perhaps I'm fearful. Perhaps I'm just lazy. But when God changes my life, I often resist. I want to retreat to my old, small, comfortable spot the way Stuart did. I want to drag things back to where they were. But God wants more for me, just as I did for Stuart. He nudges me forward and gives me grace and courage to keep going.

For several years I was a teacher in a private school. At first I taught junior high. Then I moved to third grade, and I loved it. I thought all was going well. I figured I'd be there till I retired.

Little did I suspect that a huge change was about to take place. When my contract ended, I was told that I wouldn't be returning. I was crushed, but I clung to Scripture, trusting that "in all things God works for the good of those who love him" (Romans 8:28).

I had no idea what I would be doing, but I prayed and kept my heart open. Before long, I was asked to help produce a feature film. I was shocked. I had no education in this area. But as I sought the Lord, I felt He wanted me to do it.

I had many responsibilities on this small, independent film. I found several of the locations where scenes were shot. I searched for props. I decorated sets. I made food. I was in charge of the shooting schedule. Two of my favorite parts was nurturing everyone and praying for them.

The film kept me very busy. I met wonderful people and made some great friends. I learned a lot too. At last, the project came to a close. I told God I was open to whatever else He had in mind. For now, that seems to be doing some writing and substitute teaching in the public schools.

So often I'm frightened of the unknown. I want to run back to the old life. But God has a plan, and I'm in it. He can see what lies ahead. I can't. Just like Stuart, I may deny the best by refusing to let go of the good. I must trust Him, let go of my old yard, and reach for the new opportunities He wants to give me.

Trust in the LORD and do good; dwell in the land and enjoy safe pasture (Psalm 37:3).

Consider This

Are there some new things God wants to give you that you've been resisting? What frightens you about them? How might they be a blessing? How might they expand your opportunities to serve God?

Lost and Found
Have Faith in God's Restoring Power

Praise my soul, the King of heaven;
To his feet thy tribute bring.
Ransomed, healed, restored, forgiven,
Who like me his praise should sing?

HENRY FRANCIS LYTE

When Biscuit was four, I figured she'd been an only dog long enough. I wanted to find a canine playmate for her. My search led me to a four-footed orphan I named Morgan. I took him home, and Biscuit seemed as pleased with him as I was.

But our joy didn't last. Just days later, Morgan started refusing to eat. He felt feverish too. I rushed him to the vet. His doctor quarantined him and prepared me for the worst. It looked like Morgan could have distemper. And if so, he might not make it.

Spirits sinking, I went home and broke the news to Jamie.

Jamie was a close friend and animal lover who'd been helping with Morgan's adjustment. She felt my pain. She shared it with her pastor. He promised to pray that God would heal Morgan as an expression of His love.

Those words warmed my heart, but it was still breaking. Would God answer the prayer, or would Morgan be lost to me? Whatever the outcome, I didn't want my dog to think I'd dumped him. He'd been in a shelter. I'd only had him a few short days. I feared he might feel abandoned. I called and asked to visit him. The vet was all for it.

They let me into the area where Morgan was caged. I sat and cuddled him and told him he'd have a great life if he'd just get well for me. I coaxed him to swallow a few licks of food. Meanwhile, we were being observed by a volunteer who was tending another dog. She asked what was wrong. When I explained, she said she could see that my dog adored me and felt he was going to make it.

He did. He hadn't had distemper after all. Days later, I took him home. And I rejoiced over him all the more because he'd seemed lost, and now he was found. God had restored him.

My friend Amy also rejoiced over something she'd thought lost that God restored. In her case, it was a diamond.

Amy had just learned of the death of a relative she cared deeply about. She was very distressed, uncertain if her loved one had known Christ. She'd been wrestling with her hurt, crying out to God. And then one day, she noticed her engagement ring was missing its diamond.

She'd had the ring for decades and wore it with her wedding band. Where or when the stone fell out, she wasn't sure. She searched the house, without success. She begged God to find it. And she sensed that somehow God had a lesson for her in the lost stone, a lesson that was linked to the death of her loved one.

Amy and I are part of a group who study the Bible together. She shared about the diamond. We prayed. She waited. The jewel stayed lost. A month went by.

One evening, Amy hosted a fellowship dinner in her home. When I walked through the door, her first words were, "God gave me back my diamond." She pointed to a basket used to stack old newspapers destined for the recycle bin. "It was full, so I dumped it," she said. "Then I noticed a sparkle, like a speck of glitter. I reached into the bin to find out what it was. And it was the diamond."

Amy's heart overflowed with joy for the stone because it seemed lost and now was found. And she thought she knew what God was trying to show her. If He could fish a diamond out of a trash bin, could He not restore a lost soul? Though she'd never heard the loved one she mourned profess to have faith in Christ, God could have touched his heart, even in his last moments. Nothing is impossible with Him.

Like Morgan, I've been lost and found. I suffered from a spiritual sickness called sin. God alone could heal me through Christ's death for me on the cross. But I had to receive His remedy by trusting in Christ for my salvation, confessing my need, and asking Him into my heart.

Indeed, all God's children are lost and found, fished from the trash bin of our transgressions by a loving Master who delights in restoration. We are coal He transforms into diamonds. We are gifts from God the Father to His Son...an expression of His love. He polishes us by the power of His Spirit till we shine and sparkle the way He meant us to. And when He is done, He will set us before Him and rejoice in us always.

Suppose a woman has ten silver coins and loses one. Does she not light a lamp, sweep the house and search carefully until she finds it? And when she finds it, she calls her friends and neighbors together and says, "Rejoice with me; I have found my lost coin." In the same way, I tell you, there is rejoicing in the presence of the angels of God over one sinner who repents (Luke 15:8-10).

Consider This

Have you ever lost something that God has restored? What was it? Did it surprise you? How did it impact your faith?

How might God use you as an instrument of restoration in others' lives?

Strain for the Gain

Press On in His Service

Many strokes fell tall Oaks.

John Clarke

During our early years of marriage, when Steve was first working on his parents' farm, we rented a small home down the road from them. Our dog, McPherson, lived in our fenced-in backyard. He had plenty of room to run and play. He seemed quite content, and all went well until something changed at the house next door.

Our neighbor owned a beautiful little female Australian shepherd. His dog went into heat. McPherson wanted to get to that dog. He strained and strained to jump over the fence, but he couldn't accomplish it. Then he tried to dig under, but the fence's cement border made this nearly impossible. At least, it was a lot slower going than he seemed to think he had time for.

Our home had a crawlspace that ran beneath it. There was access from the backyard—a small opening covered by a screen. McPherson found a way to pull this screen off. Then he crawled completely under the house to the front. He must have found a hole in the wood siding we knew nothing about. McPherson chewed and pulled with all his might, ripping off a huge piece of the wood to make his escape.

There wasn't a barrier separating our front yard from our neighbor's. In fact, he had no fenced-in area at all. He would tie his shepherd out front for brief intervals to relieve herself. McPherson found the object of his desire. Our neighbor found them both.

Needless to say, steps were quickly taken to keep this from happening again. McPherson strained for the gain but received only a fleeting reward. Nor were we, his masters, pleased with him, especially after our landlord yelled about the wood siding and made Steve repair the damage, quite a job in itself.

Often we, like McPherson, strain mightily for fleeting rewards that displease our Master. But Sari, our new daughter-in-law, did just the opposite. She strained for a godly gain, and her reward is ongoing.

When she was 18, Sari left home to attend college in another state. She'd been raised to believe in the Bible. She knew it teaches that sex is to be reserved for marriage. But she made a wrong choice, and it brought a big challenge. She got pregnant.

When she learned of her pregnancy, there were crucial decisions to make. She had no intention of marrying the baby's father, but she was afraid of being a single mom at such a young age. Still, she realized that having an abortion was not the answer. She knew that God cares about life, even in the womb. As the psalmist says, "For you created my inmost being; you knit me together in my mother's womb" (Psalm 139:13). She resolved to have the child, but she told her parents nothing.

And then someone offered her the money to pay for an abortion. This person urged her daily to do it. Though she'd been determined not to, it was tempting. Life could go back to what it was before she became pregnant. She walked toward the clinic, money in hand. But she stopped at the entrance, shook her fist at the door, and said, "No! I'm having this baby!"

Just after Sari turned 19, she had a beautiful little girl. She named the child Sierra. She had broken the news to her parents in her seventh month. Now she asked if she could come home to their small California town. They brought her back and helped her find a place for herself and her little girl. They and Sari's grandparents pitched in with Sierra so Sari could complete her education. She became a teacher.

Some years later, Sari and Sierra moved to Bakersfield. When Sierra was nine, Sari met our son, John. They fell in love and married, and our family grew by two. Now we have a beautiful daughter-in-law and a delightful ten-year-old granddaughter, and John has the wonderful wife God intended as well as a daughter who delights in him.

McPherson strained to achieve his own desires. Sari strained to please her Master. She knew that having a baby when she was only 19 and unmarried would be terribly hard for her. Yet she pressed on. She gained a beautiful little girl, the knowledge that she did the right thing, and the praise of her heavenly Master. Her rewards aren't fleeting like McPherson's—they're eternal.

Forgetting what is behind and straining toward what is ahead, I press on toward the goal to win the prize for which God has called me heavenward in Christ Jesus (Philippians 3:14).

Consider This

Is God nudging you to strain for the gain in an area of your life? What about it is frightening or difficult? What prize do you stand to gain if you persevere? What resources might be available to help you press on? How might you encourage others to strain for a godly reward?

Dogged Perseverance
God Loves a Persistent Pray-er

*Perseverance is the hard work you
do after you get tired of doing the
hard work you already did.*

Newt Gingrich

Morgan and Biscuit know what they want, and they are determined to get it. One thing they go after is treats. They have begging down to a fine art, and they have learned who the suckers are.

My housemate is one such easy mark. When she's cooking or eating, they plant themselves in front of her and stare. Though she may scold them (puppy eyes boring into you makes it a little hard to chew), they know she loves them and delights to please them. They stand (or sit or lay) their ground, hoping they will soon prevail. Usually, she rewards them with scraps and a bowl or plate to lick. Their dogged perseverance has paid off.

At times, Morgan's also doggedly persistent about climbing onto my lap. My boy dog loves to snuggle. He waits by my chair or bounces beside me when I first sit down at my computer. He knows he can't perch on me all day, but he wants his morning cuddle.

When I lift him up, he kisses my chin, then settles across me to bathe or snooze till I put him down. He has learned I delight to give him this good thing.

Of course, I don't just give the dogs whatever they want, whenever they want it. They must wait till the end of a meal to get table scraps. And Morgan knows to back off his bouncing and go under my desk if I command him to. I remain in charge, granting their petitions in a way that promotes discipline and character.

Our heavenly Master does the same with us.

Jesus told His disciples a parable about a widow who kept on pleading with a judge in her town to give her justice. At first the judge tried to ignore her, but he gave in at last. He didn't care about her cause; he just wanted to get her off his back. Jesus sought to encourage His disciples to persist in prayer, since our heavenly Father, unlike that judge, cares about our welfare.

My friend Claire knew this parable and believed it. She persisted in prayer for years for her niece to meet Jesus. This niece had suffered a childhood trauma that made her angry and bitter. Her mother had been snatched from her suddenly, killed in an accident. The child wondered how a loving God could let such an awful thing happen.

Claire couldn't talk to her niece very much about the Lord—the girl wouldn't let her. But she could talk to the Lord about her niece. Some days, it felt as though her prayers weren't being heard. But Claire understood that God was trustworthy and her feelings were not. She knew she was to keep praying unless God clearly told her to stop. She loved her niece dearly, and she loved the Lord dearly, and she wanted them to know each other. Years passed. The child became a young woman. Aunt Claire kept sitting at her Master's feet and pleading for a miracle.

And then the niece went through a bumpy time in her life. That rough period, the influence of a close friend, and Aunt Claire's love began to work on her heart. She was wrestling still, but her armor was cracking and God's love was seeping in. On Claire's birthday, her grown niece became a child of God.

Why did it take so many years? Humanly, we can't be sure. But we know that not just God's will, but the niece's, was involved. We know that through our perseverance, God builds character. And we know that spiritual warfare plays a part, in ways we may not guess.

The prophet Daniel experienced a delay in answered prayer that was caused by spiritual warfare. He had mourned and fasted for three weeks, seeking understanding from God (see Daniel 10). A heavenly being appeared to him and told Daniel his plea had been heard from the very first day. But this being, who had been sent to grant it, had been resisted and detained. Only after getting help with this battle could he come at last.

Clearly, persistence alone won't avail if what we beg for is wrong for us. Our all-wise Master may say no for this reason—just as I do with my dogs. And there are so many other factors, including our human will, which may affect how God answers a prayer, and when.

But Scripture shows that persistent prayer in God's will avails much and fights spiritual battles of which we're but dimly aware. And He loves to grant such requests and bless us, even as I love to bless Morgan and Biscuit.

Then Jesus told his disciples a parable to show them that they should always pray and not give up (Luke 18:1).

Consider This

Is there a long-standing prayer request you've become discouraged about? Have you asked God to show you if it's in His will? What might help you discern His answer? If it's yes, are you willing to keep praying?

The Purpose-Driven Dog
When It's God's Will, There's a Way

Every path hath a puddle.

JOHN RAY

Max, our Boston terrier, was a small and somewhat timid dog. But once he realized he was part of our family, he felt he should be our watchdog and protector. He would actually scare people off with his loud bark and mean growl.

For some reason, Max wasn't fond of John's friends when they were young teenagers. One pal, a rather large football player, stopped by our house for the first time when we weren't there. He tried to get out of his car, but Max frightened him away. I'm sure Max was also afraid, but he was determined to guard us.

There were times when his efforts were needed. Once, I opened the door to a man who seemed suspicious. His eyes roved past me and roamed the house as we talked. I was nervous and a bit uncertain about what to do. Max took over, baring his teeth and growling till the man decided to leave. I petted Max and told him what a good dog he was. His eyes lit up. He held his head high as he marched to his pillow and lay down like a tiny, proud lion. It was easy to see Max knew his purpose in life: to keep the Fleishauers safe.

Our oldest daughter, Christy, also knows her purpose in life, and she has overcome obstacles of her own to pursue it. As a child, she was timid, waiting till 18 months of age to take her first steps. It wasn't that she couldn't walk. She was just very cautious. She preferred to crawl rather than take a chance of falling and hurting herself.

Christy was also quiet and shy. Her teachers used to tell us she would always have the right answer, but she would never raise her hand. They admitted she got left out of special programs because they simply forgot about her. I would often see her standing in a group of kids at church or school. They'd be deep in conversation, but she wouldn't be saying a word.

But there was an area where Christy shone. It was music. She began playing French horn in fourth grade and kept on right through high school. She played in marching band, concert band, and the Kern County Honor Band. She was shy about talking to people, but she could play her horn before thousands.

Christy earned her college degree in music. After graduating, she felt led of God to become a music teacher. This required not just talking with students, but dealing with parents, school staff, and administrators. She was still very shy, but she was determined to fulfill God's purpose for her. Her deep desire to follow her calling motivated her to learn to talk in public. She developed great relationships with students and adults alike. After teaching music in a private school for three years, Christy entered a program to get her teaching credential and become a classroom teacher.

Max knew his purpose and didn't let size or timidity keep him from serving his masters. Christy didn't let shyness stop her from fulfilling God's call. God has a purpose for each of us. If it's His will, He'll provide a way if we will just obey, step out, and trust in Him.

I can do everything through him who gives me strength (Philippians 4:13).

Consider This

Do you know what God's calling is on your life right now? Have you stepped out, or are you hanging back? If you're hesitating, why is that? How might you better fulfill God's purpose for you, now and in the future?

Part III

Meal Choices

If a Dog Could Eat Forever

Our Appetites Can Get Us into Trouble

Greed oft o'erreaches itself.

Aesop

For most of her life, Gracie ate like a vacuum cleaner—sucking food in so fast she barely had time to chew. She'd lick her bowl for every trace, down to the dust particles. Then, she'd look up at me, hoping beyond hope that I'd give her another scoop. Maybe two or three times a year, I'd relent and let her have a few more morsels.

Occasionally, as I watched her inhale her food as if it were a kibble-eating contest, I wondered what would happen if I dumped the whole 20-pound bag of dog food into a bucket and let her eat as much as she wanted. Would she chow down until she passed out? Would she gobble and gobble until she ballooned into a freaky 500 pound sumo dog?

I never tried this experiment. As her master, I chose to set the limits of her food intake: not too little, lest she starve, and not too much, lest she become obese. I gave her what I thought was the right amount to keep her at a healthy weight. I hope she realized that, as she looked at me with those big, begging eyes of hers. *Please, give me MORE!*

Too often, I look at God like that. I flash big, begging eyes toward heaven right after God has given me my daily bread. He knows just what I need to keep me spiritually healthy and growing in Him. But I grumble and plead for more, instead of being satisfied with enough.

The children of Israel had to learn to be satisfied with enough when God gave them their daily manna in the desert. In Exodus 16, Moses told the people, "This is what the LORD has commanded: 'Each one is to gather as much as he needs. Take an omer for each person you have in your tent'" (Exodus 16:16). The Israelites obeyed, and though some gathered more and others less, they all had just enough. Moses also warned them not to hoard their manna till the next day. Those who tried found their day-old manna smelly and filled with maggots. God wanted His people to trust Him for their daily bread on a daily basis…just the way dogs instinctively do with their masters, and small children do with their parents.

When I was a child, I learned the Lord's Prayer. One of the easier lines to remember was, "Give us each day our daily bread" (Luke 11:3). It rolled off my tongue easily when I was ten—before I was into acquiring money and material things. But as an adult, am I willing to pray this with conviction? Am I willing to ask, "Dear God, just give me enough for today and don't let me have too much of a good thing?" If I'm honest, more often I grumble and gripe. "Is this all I get, Lord? Just one cup of food in the morning and one cup at night? Is that all the money, power, and fame You're going to dole out to me? I want *more*. I can handle it. I deserve it!"

Like my dog, I'm blessed to have a Master who provides all my needs. I have never lacked the basic necessities of life. I've always had food to eat, clothes to wear, and a roof over my head. I've even had extras, such as cars, bikes, watches, microwaves, gym memberships, TVs, PCs, VCRs, DVDs, CDs, IRAs….

In my infrequent moments of epiphany, when I'm fully focused on Christ, I realize I have a wonderful life. But as soon as I blink my eyes off God, I return to my default position as a human being lured by fleshly desires. I don't want just what's in my dish—I want the whole 20-pound bag of food, and I want it now. I want God to pour out *all* the blessings so I can vacuum them up to my heart's content. Spend till I bust. Buy stuff I don't need to fill the emptiness in my heart. I've been taught all my life that more is a good thing.

But perhaps God sees it differently. Perhaps He knows that I don't need more—I just need more of Him.

Just as Gracie might eat until she hurt herself, God knows I might spend and consume until I hurt myself. I have to trust that His wisdom in the daily care and feeding of Kris far exceeds my wisdom.

"Thank You, Lord, that You know exactly how much of a good thing Your children need. Thank You for my daily bread!"

Give me neither poverty nor riches, but give me only my daily bread. Otherwise, I may have too much and disown you and say, "Who is the Lord*?" Or I may become poor and steal, and so dishonor the name of my God (Proverbs 30:8-9).*

Consider This

Are there some areas in your life where you want more? How do you think this would benefit you? How might it be detrimental?

Has there been a time when the old adage "less is more" was true for you? Why was that so?

More than He Could Chew

To Hoard Is Human; to Share, Divine

Much would have more.

JOHN CLARKE

When the dogs were younger, their sharp little teeth made short work of many a chew toy. But there was one type of chew bone that seemed to last longer. It was specially made so it wouldn't sliver and stick in their throats, the way real bones could. I bought the bones in pairs, one for each pup.

Morgan had a different notion.

A frequent scenario went like this. Biscuit mouthed a bone and settled down to chew. Morgan saw and snatched her prize away. Biscuit trotted off and grabbed a second bone to gnaw. Morgan dropped his bone and yanked away her new one. She went for the bone he'd abandoned. He grabbed it back…and on it went. Morgan's mission was keeping both bones for himself.

Trouble was, he could only chew one bone at a time.

I've realized that I, too, often grab more bones than I can chew. One place my hoarding instinct rears its ugly head is with my roses.

I have always loved roses, and not just because this flower is my middle name. Growing up, my parents had bushes in our garden. Vases of these blooms brightened up the house. They smelled lovely too. When I bought my own home, I put roses in also. I loved to cut and arrange them.

Sharing them sometimes came a bit harder.

One year, my Master nudged me to take roses to my Bible class. It was the last meeting before our summer break. We needed prizes for those who'd memorized the most Scripture. God told me to offer some of my "rose bones"…not just any blooms, but those I liked best.

I had lots of roses. My favorite bushes would grow more flowers that year. But oh, how I fought with myself to let go of those bones. My patient Master did not give up. He tugged at my heart and urged me to lay them at His feet by sharing them. At last, I did.

I've amassed other bones…porcelain figurines and art glass. I have filled display cabinets. Yet, I buy more. I'm not saying it's wrong to collect things, but how much is too much?

Our culture teaches us to be consummate consumers. It says two bones, or twenty, are better than one. But God's Word gives a very different message. Jesus warned of the danger of hoarding things. He told a parable of a rich man whose storehouses overflowed. But he didn't think to share his bones. He planned to build bigger storehouses still, so he could pile up more. Then he learned he would die that night and have to leave his bones behind.

Piling up more bones than I can chew won't help me any more than it helped Morgan. But God says there's one thing I can store up to my heart's content. That's spiritual treasure—and one way I can gain it is by giving of my bones.

Do not store up for yourselves treasures on earth, where moth and rust destroy, and where thieves break in and steal. But store up for yourselves treasures in heaven, where moth and rust do not destroy, and where thieves do not break in and steal. For where your treasure is, there your heart will be also (Matthew 6:19-21).

Consider This

Which bones are you most tempted to hoard? What makes them difficult to share? Are there bones you wish others would share with you? What are they?

What's Up, Doc?
Daily Helpings of Scripture Are Essential to Health

God heals, and the Doctor takes the Fees.

BENJAMIN FRANKLIN

Gracie was the kind of dog who never needed a vet. She was 100 percent pure "mutt"—most likely the love child of a German shepherd and a corgi. This crossbreeding produced a hardy, robust little pooch who was almost never sick. Then, a couple of years ago, Gracie started to drink and urinate excessively. She ate ravenously, but lost weight and grew weak. We had her examined. Diagnosis—diabetes.

Gracie's vet put her on a special, high-fiber prescription dog food. He also ordered insulin injections. He told me I'd need to give her two shots a day for the rest of her life. If she didn't get her insulin, she'd die. But disciplined medical maintenance could help keep her disease in check…at least for a while.

I, too, needed a daily dose of medicine to keep my disease in check. My ailments were panic attacks and depression. They came upon me insidiously, like the diabetes came upon Gracie. At first, I didn't even know I was sick. I tried to ignore the symptoms.

But like Gracie's thirst and weight loss, they heightened. I found it increasingly distressing to drive on crowded freeways, sit in crowded theaters, or fly in an airplane. Dread attached itself to me like superglue. Waking up each morning was a huge chore. I tried going to counselors—even took a few antidepressants. Nothing worked.

Then I prayed to God. I begged for mercy. "Help me. I have nowhere else to turn."

The Great Physician examined me and revealed His diagnosis. In my case, the problem was at least partly spiritual…a disease of the heart. Like Gracie, I needed lifelong medicine—daily doses of God's Word.

Though I had always known the Bible was good for me, I had never viewed it as essential to life. But I was so weary of being weary that I began a daily program of disciplined Scripture reading and memorization. The results were not immediate, but in time my symptoms subsided.

These days I can once again bear to sit with my fellow L.A. drivers in übertraffic. Crowded theaters and airplanes pose no problem for me. Most of the time, I wake up looking forward to a new day.

Still, I recognize I'm not totally cured, anymore than Gracie was. I'm still prone to anxiety and depression. When I get too busy and neglect my daily injection of Scripture, it's not long till the dual dragons of worry and panic are back panting at my door. Luckily, I know how to chase them off—just take my remedy again.

Indeed, our Good Shepherd and Divine Doctor would prescribe daily doses of His Word to all who are in His care. It's our medicine to save, preserve, and deliver us. Feast on it—and live!

My soul is weary with sorrow; strengthen me according to your word (Psalm 119:28).

Consider This

Do you have a regular time each day when you read and study God's Word? If not, what is keeping you from it? How might you prioritize your life to make room for Bible study?

One Dog's Chicken
God Withholds Things for a Reason

One man's meat is another man's poison.

OSWALD DYKES

Biscuit has always had a sensitive digestive system. As a puppy, she had bouts of colitis. Her vet put her on a special prescription dry food. In time, she outgrew the condition. When Morgan joined the family, I was able to feed them both the same store-bought kibble. But Biscuit's tummy continued to be a bit touchy…especially with chicken.

Biscuit loved chicken. Sadly, it did not love her. If she ate it, she wound up wearing the repercussions. I knew from the streaks on her normally white furry bottom that this food did not agree with her. But I doubt that Biscuit connected this favorite treat with its end result. Though Morgan had no trouble with it, I stopped giving chicken to either dog. I knew Biscuit wouldn't understand why she couldn't have it and he could.

God handles His children a little differently than I do my dogs. He puts different things on our various plates of life. He wants us to trust that if someone else gets chicken and we don't, it's for our best. But I don't always do that.

One of my ongoing pleas for chicken involves my writing career. I've wanted more worldly success. I've yearned for a bestseller. I've cried "no fair" when God wouldn't put that chicken on my plate. I've grumbled and grown bitter at God when a novel I wrote languished in the hinterlands of book sales while other titles soared.

But all the while, I secretly wondered if the chicken I begged for might give me the runs—spiritually and otherwise. When the pressure mounts, I tend to tense up and get sick. Perhaps more success would ramp up the professional pace of my life to a level I couldn't handle. I have also struggled with issues of pride. I've been tempted to depend on my own strength, not God's. If I got my chicken, would it mess up my spiritual digestion in these areas?

I shared my struggles with a ministry partner. He told me God wouldn't hurt me. Did that mean he, too, questioned whether I could handle chicken? I cringed at the thought, but just months later, something happened that proved his comment insightful.

I'd been procrastinating on starting the third volume of a fiction trilogy. A publisher wasn't in place. I felt burned out. I wanted some assurance that my efforts would be "worth it"—by my definition. I felt God was nudging me to get busy, but I resisted His prodding.

Finally, I went to work...too late. An opportunity arose for a major book club to offer the trilogy in one volume, but I would need to finish in four short months, and I didn't even have an outline for the third book yet.

Someone else might have digested that chicken, but I feared I couldn't. The schedule seemed too tight and the pressure too intense. After seeking God and counseling with others, I felt compelled, reluctantly, to turn the offer down.

That opportunity may resurface, or it may be gone forever. What I hope will remain is the lesson my Master taught me. Had I stopped drooling over other people's chicken and spent my time craving what God had placed on my own plate, I might have been prepared to receive the blessing He offered.

Dogs and people don't remain the same. They change and grow. What was hurtful at one point in our life may be fine later on.

These days, Biscuit can handle a little chicken, and I let her have some. My Master is watching for my growth as well, and He will adjust what's on my plate for my good and His glory, if I will trust in Him.

"For I know the plans I have for you," declares the LORD, "plans to prosper you and not to harm you, plans to give you hope and a future" (Jeremiah 29:11).

Consider This

Is there some chicken you've been begging God for that He hasn't given you? Why do you want it? How might it change your life? Might it be hard to handle? If so, why?

Opportunities
Seize What God Offers

Gather ye rosebuds while ye may,
Old Time is still a-flying:
And this same flower that smiles to-day,
To-morrow will be dying.

ROBERT HERRICK

Stuart loves to run and play, so we've given him the opportunity to run free on the farm. He can dash all over the yard and orchard as long as he comes when he's called. He's been trained that way, and he understands this. But he doesn't always obey.

One time we let Stuart run loose while we were in the yard. We got busy, and before we knew it, he was out of sight. We called and called him. He didn't return. Finally, Steve, Karen, and I all took different vehicles and rushed off in search of him. We drove all over the farm, calling him as we went. I headed down the road. As I was passing a neighbor's house, I saw someone walking Stuart up to their front door. I claimed him, thanked the folks who found him, and headed back. But by the time we all got home, dinner was burned, and Steve was late to a meeting.

Stuart was given an opportunity, but he abused it. He disobeyed and didn't come back when he should have. While we didn't kick him out of the family, we did take away this privilege for a short time so he would learn a lesson.

Thinking of Stuart's situation reminds me of a special class in one of the schools where I substitute teach. It's an "opportunity class" for students on the verge of being expelled. They must stay in one classroom, separated from the rest of the student body, unable to participate in regular school activities. They eat by themselves and travel to and from school on a separate schedule. If they improve and show that they can follow school rules, they're allowed to rejoin their schoolmates once their time in the class is over. If not, they must suffer the consequences…just like Stuart.

I have really enjoyed substituting in this class. It has given me a chance to work with students one-on-one. I recall two pupils in particular. They both had a great deal of potential, but they squandered their opportunity. They didn't follow the rules. As a consequence, one lost the privilege of participating in graduation exercises. The other student was expelled from school altogether. It wasn't that they couldn't do it. They just wouldn't.

God gives us opportunities too. You could say that life is an opportunity class. We have an opportunity to be delivered from sin by accepting Christ as our personal Savior. We have a chance to be cleansed and forgiven based on what He did for us. If we take this opportunity, we become members of God's family and will not be expelled but will spend eternity with Him. Once we seize that opportunity, God gives us many others. But taking them, and obtaining the blessings they bring, involves obedience.

When our children were little, I was mostly a stay-at-home mom. I watched many of my friends return to school and get their teaching credentials. I said that was fine for them, but I would never do that.

Never say never.

Years later, I felt my heavenly Father telling me to go back and finish my education so I could teach. Our children were getting older, and Christy would soon be in college. Sending her to the private Christian university of her choice would take funds beyond our means. If I taught, I could earn the extra money. Friends encouraged me, and Steve and I decided I should try it.

Seizing this opportunity proved a huge task. It was quite hard on all of us. But I graduated and got a teaching job. This led to many new opportunities and blessings. One stands out.

I had a student in one of my classes who struggled with his reading. When he read out loud, he spoke ever so slowly, sounding out each word. The rest of the class was very supportive, but this little guy felt terrible. He felt as though he was letting his whole class down.

I talked with him and offered him the opportunity to work with me at recess. He agreed, seeming a bit nervous but excited too.

I had done some studying about a particular visual-perceptual disorder. According to the information I had, it could cause reading difficulties. After talking with my student, I suspected he might have this problem. We tried a few things. At first, nothing was helping. And then, something did. All at once, he started reading fluidly, and with expression. Once his problem was addressed, he began to read with a confidence I had never seen in him.

I asked him if he'd like to read for the class again. He was eager to do so. When he finished, they all cheered him. It was one of my best teaching days. If I hadn't obeyed God and seized the opportunity to teach, I would have missed this blessing.

Way back in the book of Genesis, we read that God gave a man named Abram some incredible opportunities. Abram had a chance to be a great man, to be the father of a great nation, and to be a source of blessing to all the earth's peoples. But to gain these opportunities, Abram had to obey, just like Stuart. Just like Stuart, he had to listen when his Master called. He had to leave his family, his people, and his country and go to the land God would show him.

Abram did what God asked. God renamed him Abraham. He became the father of the Hebrew nation and the ancestor of the Messiah.

Obey your Master, seize the opportunities He offers, and enter into His joy!

The LORD had said to Abram, "Leave your country, your people and your father's household and go to the land I will show you. I will make you into a great nation and I will bless you; I will make your name great, and you will be a blessing. I will bless those who bless you, and whoever curses you I will curse; and all peoples on earth will be blessed through you" (Genesis 12:1-3).

Consider This

What opportunities is God offering you right now? What steps of obedience must you take to seize them? Have you done so? If not, what is holding you back? If so, what has been the result?

Tummy Love

Are You Chasing the Food Bowls of This World?

Whose bread I eat, his song I sing.

PROVERB

It's been said that the way to a man's heart is through his stomach. It's the way to a dog's heart too. Morgan and Biscuit are constantly selling their birthright for a mess of pottage. Okay, so it's not pottage; it's table scraps. Same difference. When my housemate has food, my dogs desert me and hang out with her.

Imagine, if you will, this scenario. I am drinking my morning coffee. I've just let the pups out and fed them their daily kibble. Kibble I have gone to the store and bought out of my own pocket, mind you! Having dined, my pooches sprawl at my feet.

Then my housemate stumbles into the kitchen. She heads for the fridge and pulls out the fixings of her favorite breakfast. The dogs make a beeline for this new food source and watch as she mixes yogurt and berries. They park at her feet, eyes glued on her, till she gives them her bowl to lick. If I call them back, they act deaf. They only come if I insist…grudgingly, at that. So much for loyalty.

The same scenario might be replayed at lunch or dinner, especially if my housemate is cooking, which she does more often than I do. My little beggars forsake me to wait for her handouts. The momentary pleasures of this world lure them off to where the bowl is fuller. Never mind all the vet bills I've paid and the care I've provided. Never mind that I'm their true master. Tummy love prevails. Ah, the fickleness of canines.

Ah, the fickleness of humans.

My dogs' behavior has been a reminder that I've not always been faithful, either. I have failed to appreciate those who cared most for me…my parents. This was especially true in my midteens. I'd developed an eating disorder and resented their efforts to intervene. Though my illness had complicated psychological causes and ramifications, I'd slipped into trouble at least partly by sitting at the feet of a cultural idol—thinness. I longed for the food bowls of popularity and attractiveness. My parents tried to call me back, but I didn't want to come. I saw them as overcontrolling. I thought they should back off and let me have the appearance and identity I wanted.

We had many clashes, but one stands out. I stormed out the door in a huff to go exercise. There were tennis courts a short distance away. I climbed on my bike, tennis racket in hand, and started down the driveway. I couldn't balance both the bike and the racket. The bike tipped over and I went with it, slamming my chin into the asphalt.

I stumbled back into the house, screaming, dripping blood and spitting tooth chips. My faithful parents rushed their prodigal to a hospital emergency room. A doctor stitched up the gash beneath my chin, but that was just the beginning. I'd fractured nine teeth. I needed weeks of dental work, during which my dad fixed meals for me in a blender. Despite how I'd fought them, my parents stood by me and saw me through the whole miserable episode.

As a child of God, I now have a Father greater even than my earthly parents. He has promised to care for me for all eternity. He meets my needs, is with me always, and guarantees me an inheritance that is priceless and imperishable. He is worthy of nothing less than my undivided loyalty.

And yet, the food bowls of this world still beckon. Though I've never totally turned from Him, I've been guilty of tummy love in smaller ways. All too often I'm more eager to sit at the Internet's feet than God's. I've poured hours into checking out the latest deals on eBay or searching for the best buy on a new appliance or combing websites for some collectible I wanted. And when I do curl up in my easy chair to read God's Word and pray, I usually leave my computer on, and I'm tempted to come if AOL calls, "You've got mail."

Jesus told a parable about a young man who was chasing tummy love. He asked for an early inheritance, then left home and squandered it. Alone and penniless, he realized his error. And so the prodigal returned, hoping he might be allowed to be a servant in his father's household. But his father told the servants to drape the boy in his best robe, kill the fatted calf, and prepare a banquet in his honor—rejoicing that his son had been restored to him (see Luke 15:11-22).

Deep down, my dogs know who their master is. In the end, they return to me. I return to my Master too…and He receives me. He's not fickle, like I am. He doesn't engage in tummy love. Despite my weakness, He is faithful forever, and His love is everlasting.

You, O Lord, are a compassionate and gracious God, slow to anger, abounding in love and faithfulness (Psalm 86:15).

Consider This

What are some ways you have engaged in tummy love? How has it affected your life? What might you change to be more faithful to God and to others?

Three Flavors of Bark
Will the Words You Speak Nourish Others?

*Words—so innocent and powerless as they
are, as standing in a dictionary, how potent
for good and evil they become, in the hands
of one who knows how to combine them!*

NATHANIEL HAWTHORNE

Like most dogs, Gracie barked. I'm sure if she'd had human intelligence and could speak, she'd have told me exactly why she barked and what she was trying to communicate when she did so. "Dogs Speak English Day" never happened, so when Gracie passed on, her secrets died with her. But, from my point of view, Gracie did three kinds of barking: bad or worthless, amusing or neutral, and good or precious.

Gracie barking in the backyard at 2 AM for no apparent reason was annoying or bad barking. It rarely happened, but on a night when her woofing jolted me out of bed and sent me into the yard with a flashlight in search of a nonexistent intruder, I was a little put out. I'd look at Gracie and ask, "What were you barking at?" She would stare mutely at me, wagging her tail, grinning at the success of rousing me from my slumber. I'd put her in the kitchen and then try to get back to sleep, wondering how I was going to be coherent at the important meeting I had scheduled early in the morning. I'm sure Gracie's reasons for barking were valid from her perspective, but to my weary mind, they were worthless.

Sometimes, when I was gardening in the backyard, Gracie would do some amusing or neutral barking. As I pulled weeds, she would suddenly erupt in a barking fit. I'd look to find her focused intently up into the branches of our big elm tree, furiously hurling dog epithets at a cocky squirrel that merrily munched on an acorn safely above Gracie's head. I found this kind of barking amusing. I could see why she was barking and at whom. I could guess what was probably going through her doggie brain. And her barking didn't bug me, even though it was of no benefit. My writer's mind concocted all kinds of human words Gracie would be saying. "Come on down here and fight like a dog!" Or "This tree's on my turf, squirrel! Beat it!" I thought of Gracie as a lady, so I didn't think she'd have said anything worse than that.

Then there was a third kind of barking Gracie did—good barking—barking that pleased me. Gracie would often lie on the hardwood floor of our living room while my wife and I were reading at night. While we heard nothing more than a steady chorus of crickets chirping, Gracie would abruptly perk up her head and woof. She'd get up, go over to the front door, and bark some more. More often than not, this signaled a stranger walking up our driveway. My wife appreciated this about Gracie because it was an early warning system that alerted her, especially when she was home alone at night. Gracie got so good at this that she could tell the difference between the automobiles of friends and strangers. When a friend drove up in a car she'd grown accustomed to, she wouldn't bark, but merely whine positively and wag her tail. When a stranger's car pulled up and parked outside, she'd let loose a few warning barks. It was like having a gate monitor at the base of the driveway to signal us as to who was arriving. As Gracie grew deaf, we truly began to miss this good-and-precious-barking feature of our dog.

Like Gracie, I speak all day long. It would be sobering if each day a log was kept of everything that came out of my mouth. At the end of each day, I'd have to submit this log to God for review. And what if He judged my word output the way I judged Gracie's barking? From God's point of view, Kris would either have spoken or written: bad or worthless words, amusing or neutral words, or good or precious words.

I don't keep such a log, but God always lets me know what He thinks of my words in ways that I can understand. Just as I scolded Gracie for bad barking or praised her for good barking, the Holy Spirit convicts or commends me in similar fashion.

Any married person knows how a few bad words spewed to a spouse can cause a world of trouble at home. It took days to recover from telling my wife, "It's hard to live with a person like you." Instead of reacting to her with precious words of forgiveness and love (as God commands), I instead chose to *bark* in a mean-spirited way. My harsh words probably annoyed God as much as Gracie's worthless 2 AM barking bothered me.

Then, there are the amusing words that come forth from my mouth. I'm thinking of the bedtime stories I make up for my son, Skye. The latest is about a flying train he and his stuffed dog can climb into, one that will take him anywhere he wishes. I don't necessarily teach great biblical truths while talking about this winged train, but my boy and I find it amusing, and I'd like to think God does too.

And then, there are the times I utter not what is worthless or merely amusing, but what is good and precious. Last year I was invited to speak at the Veritas Forum at USC. It's a three-day event on college campuses to foster discussion about spiritual issues in a variety of disciplines, from science to politics to the arts. I was supposed to give a talk on the power of story and film. I was nervous and didn't know what to expect. When I'm like this, I pray and seek God more than usual because I know I can't talk in front of 300 people in my own strength. I asked God to take over. I prayed that what would come out of my mouth that evening would be precious to His ears, not worthless. One of the things I spoke about was the need for filmmakers and screenwriters to take responsibility for the stories they tell. I believe that modern-day audiences look to film to feed their hungry hearts and souls in the way that the masses once looked to religion. After my talk was over, a goodly number of film students came up and thanked me for opening their eyes to the need to produce good and precious food for audiences as opposed to bad or junk food for the soul.

I felt honored to have served God and had an inner joy from knowing I spoke the truth that night. The Holy Spirit confirmed in my heart that my words were precious and good, not bad barking or mere amusing or neutral anecdotes.

When Gracie pleased me with good barking, I gave her a pat on the head and said, "Good dog!" I hope when I speak or write good words, God will pat me on the head and say, "Well done, good and faithful servant!" (Matthew 25:21).

If you utter what is precious, and not what is worthless, you shall serve as my mouth (Jeremiah 15:19 NRSV).

Consider This

How have your words impacted your hearers when they were good or precious? How have people been affected when your words were amusing or neutral? What has been the result when you spoke bad or worthless words to others?

If God kept a log of your words each day, how do you think He'd judge them?

Please Don't Eat the Pillows
God Can Help You Handle Stress

Gluttony is an emotional escape, a
sign that something is eating us.

PETER DE VRIES

When I brought Biscuit home, she was just a puppy. Like human babies, puppies teethe on things. During Biscuit's first day in my office, she gnawed on a mouse. Well, actually, it was the cord to my computer mouse. I bought a new one and started to practice prevention. I got Biscuit chew toys she could teethe on to her heart's content. I tried to keep other things she might chew out of reach. But there was one notable exception…pillows.

In my house, the kitchen and den are really one big room, separated by an open passageway. I let my two cats, and now Biscuit, hang out there when I wasn't home. They could get to their food and water, and there was an added perk. The den had a built-in couch of plaster padded with cushions and pillows. I let the cats sleep on it, or cuddle with me while I watched TV. I figured Biscuit would love curling up there too.

She did. Trouble was, she also chewed the pillows.

I should have gated Biscuit in the kitchen, put a dog bed down for her, and been done with the matter. But I didn't. Truth be told, I was probably looking to replace the pillows. They'd been left in the house years before by its previous owners, and I was tired of them. Biscuit's chewing gave me just the excuse I needed. I did try removing them when I was gone and replacing them when I returned. But the pillows were huge and a pain to maneuver. "No chew" spray did no good, either. I figured I'd live with ratty pillows till Biscuit stopped teething and then redo the couch completely.

Time passed. As my dog neared her second birthday, she still hadn't totally stopped chewing. But I was ready. I chose new couch fabric and had tougher, smaller pillows made. When I found slight damage to one of them, I redesigned the corners to be harder to bite. It worked. Biscuit let those pillows be.

Some time afterward, her trainer reminded me of something I'd apparently forgotten. He had guessed Biscuit's chewing wasn't triggered only by a need to teethe. He'd felt it was also a stress response. I kept her close when I was home, so when I left, she got uptight. She chewed to relieve her anxiety. The pillows were her pacifier.

Maybe acorns don't fall far from the tree. I, Biscuit's mom, also chew to relieve my stress. My pacifier is food, especially sweets. If I'm stuck on a story, or mildly depressed, or nervous in a social situation, I am apt to gnaw on something. And at times my chewing has been destructive too.

This habit got badly out of hand in the years I worked as a staff writer for an animation studio. The readily accessible food machines were a huge temptation. So were the goodies people brought to the office and left by the coffee machine. And then, there were the once-a-month group birthday parties, complete with huge cakes. At one point, I had gained close to 40 pounds. Ouch!

Both Biscuit and I were dealing with stress in an unproductive way. We were dulling the symptoms without addressing their cause. And so the symptoms kept coming back, and we kept repeating the destructive behavior. But Biscuit only hurt a few pillows. I risked my health.

For both of us, there was a better answer. In Biscuit's case, it involved conditioning. Her trainer had suggested a solution, but I didn't follow through. He'd urged me to put her in a room alone for short periods when I was home so she'd get more used to being somewhere without me. If she stopped stressing when I was gone, she might stop chewing too. But I liked having Biscuit near me, so I didn't do as he'd advised. And I literally paid the price.

I, too, had better options to handle my anxiety. I could have nibbled raw vegetables rather than sweets. I could have let off steam by exercising not my teeth but my body. And I could have calmed myself by chewing on God's Word and His promises.

But I didn't, and don't—not most of the time. Why not? Why don't I choose God's Living Bread over ice cream and chips? Why don't I look to Him when I'm stressed, instead of in the fridge or the cupboard? Could this be conditioning too, the wrong kind? And if so, can my heavenly Trainer help me change it?

God says He will never leave us, which is something I can't promise Biscuit. He urges us to give our cares to Him. He says we can talk to Him anytime, and we don't even need an appointment. He guarantees His Word will fill and satisfy us like no earthly food can. And it's one comfort food that will pile on peace, not pounds.

Do not be anxious about anything, but in everything, by prayer and petition, with thanksgiving, present your requests to God. And the peace of God, which transcends all understanding, will guard your hearts and your minds in Christ Jesus (Philippians 4:6-7).

Consider This

What are the chief stressors in your life? How do you handle them? Do your methods work, or might some of them prove destructive? What might you do differently, with God's help? Are there others you could join with for prayer and support?

Part IV

To Heel or
Not to Heel

Rub-a-Dub-Ugh!
We Need Regular Spiritual Baths

Create in me a clean heart, O God;
and renew a right spirit within me.

PSALM 51:10 KJV

Like all dogs and small children, if Gracie had been left to herself, she never would have taken a bath. Of course, she diligently licked herself and whiled away many an afternoon gnawing at her fur for fleas. She'd occasionally flip belly up and rub herself on the concrete in a canine version of dry cleaning. She shed some hair that way and got rid of some caked-on dirt—but it wasn't good enough for me. My standards of cleanliness were higher than Gracie's. It was I who decided when, where, and how Gracie would bathe. If I could smell her D.O. (doggie odor)—if a pat on the head brought forth a cloud of dust—it was time for my dog to meet soap and water.

Gracie never volunteered for a bath. Whenever she saw me coming with the dreaded purple bath leash in hand, she'd high-tail it in the other direction. I had to grab her, carry her outside, and leash her to the railing. Then I'd turn on the hose and wet her down. When her fur soaked up water and clung to her ribs, she looked somewhat embarrassed—like we would if we were caught outside in our underwear. But she endured it while I lathered her up. She flinched when I poured water on her face, or if the water was cold. She'd try to walk off—but the leash prevented her from wandering. She couldn't leave until I deemed the cleansing was complete. My standards overruled her desires.

My wife's standards overruled mine.

When I was single, my roommate and I thought we had a reasonably clean house. After all, we washed the floors and dishes as necessary. We picked up our clothes—sometimes. We were comfortable with our standards.

Then I got married. It was eye-opening. When my wife moved in, she found dirt and disorder that had heretofore been invisible to the male eye. To this day, almost seven years later, I am still learning the difference between "married clean" and "bachelor clean." If I don't do my part to keep the house married clean, our relationship suffers.

God also has His standards of "clean," and they're higher than our human ones. Only He is truly good, and compared to Him, all humans have sinned and fallen short of His cleanliness. We may think we're clean in our fine clothes, fancy cars, and luxury homes—but in God's eyes, we're pitiful, poor, blind, naked, and just plain icky. Even if we tried, there is nothing we could do to remove the stench and stain of sin. The only soap and water that can cleanse us to God's standard is Christ's blood. And while our initial cleansing and rebirth into God's family is a onetime event, we still need the daily purification of repentance and confession to keep us sweet smelling and clean in order to stay in close relationship with Him.

God's cleansing of me, His leading me by the leash of the Holy Spirit to acknowledge and confess my sins, is often unpleasant. The Spirit's convicting power makes me flinch the way the hose did Gracie. Most of the time, I think the purification should stop a lot sooner than God does. Unlike my dog, I could resist and pull away.

But I've learned that my Master is wiser than I am. It is to my benefit to endure my spiritual bathing until He deems me clean.

Gracie might not have relished the cleansing process, but she certainly loved the result. When I shut off the hose and let her loose at last, she romped with joy. She seemed proud of her clean coat. She showed it off, dashing round and round in mad little circles, shaking her body to whip off the excess water. It gave me pleasure to watch her appreciate what I'd done for her—something she couldn't have done for herself.

I've known the same joy when I've had a spiritual bath...joy based not on my feelings but on God's promise to forgive me. I do my own version of romping around and dashing in mad little circles. My spirit, once weighed down by sin, is lifted on eagle's wings. Then I realize Jesus did for me what I could never have done for myself—and I hope it gives Him pleasure as I give Him praise.

Have mercy on me, O God, according to your unfailing love; according to your great compassion blot out my transgressions. Wash away all my iniquity and cleanse me from my sin (Psalm 51:1-2).

Consider This

Do you acknowledge the difference between your idea of cleanliness and God's? What's your spiritual hygiene like on a daily basis? How does this affect your walk with the Lord?

God's Grooming Tips
Use Care When You Confront

*Sin begins as a spider's web and
becomes as a ship's rope.*

Rabbi Akiba

Biscuit has a thick, white, woolly coat that's a beauty to behold. When she's freshly bathed and groomed, she looks like a cover dog. But you'd think by its color and length that her fur would be a nightmare to maintain.

Actually, it's not. A book on her breed, the American Eskimo, says these dogs have self-cleaning coats. What this means is, the coat has a texture that repels dirt. Biscuit doesn't need constant bathing. But she does need frequent brushing and combing to remove loose fur and tangles.

Biscuit hasn't always relished her beauty appointments. She hates it when her hair gets pulled. In her younger days, she nipped a groomer who was brushing her after a bath. He thought she was being a baby, but I disagreed. I felt that perhaps she had sensitive skin and he was a little too rough.

The best way to make grooming easy on Biscuit is to keep up with it. Otherwise, a small tangle may turn into a mat or clump.

But, imperfect master that I am, I don't always get the job done. If my failure results in a large, stubborn mat, I don't even try to work with it first, in the recommended fashion.* I snip it with scissors.

One day, that process backfired.

I had found a large mat just behind Biscuit's ear. Impatient to clip it, I grabbed the scissors at hand. It had pointed ends, not the blunted ones I should have used. In the process of trying to snip the mat, I nipped her skin as well. In this spot the skin was loose. I could actually look down into the hole I had created. I was horrified!

Luckily, Biscuit seemed in no discomfort. Still, I whisked her straight off to the vet. He treated the wound to make sure it would not get infected. Then, instead of stitches, he used a special substance to seal her skin together. She healed fine, thanks to her wonderful doctor, who fixed the grooming mess I'd made.

I have also made spiritual grooming messes by using the wrong tools and timing. One such mess involved a close friend I'll call Kate.

Kate was struggling with a knotty problem in her life, and it was growing worse. We had talked about it, and she was wrestling with the situation. But on this day, I grew impatient. I felt there was a "mat" involved, and I used verbal scissors. I sent Kate an email whose words were sharp instead of blunted. They nipped her heart. She drew back, wounded and bleeding.

Though I'd meant well, I'd blown it. I had forced my own opinions on another. I had been too rough. And my timing had been awful. Nor was Kate the only one hurting; I was too. I feared I'd destroyed our friendship. Kate was in no shape to talk, so I whisked her to our Great Physician in my heart. Following His prescription, I emailed an apology, confessing that my comments had been out of line. I hoped my repentance might soothe the sting I had caused. Our wonderful heavenly Doctor healed her wound with His love and sealed the hole in our friendship with forgiveness. In His time,

---

* For suggestions on mat removal, consult your groomer, vet, or written material on dog care.

the Master we both share combed her problem out with a skill I could never match.

God is the perfect groomer!

He whitened our spiritual fur once for all time through Christ's death for our sins. He sent His Spirit to tend and groom us daily. He seeks to comb out our spiritual tangles before they become big and clumpy. His touch is gentle, His tools precise, His timing and technique unequalled. Even when we resist and our fur gets more matted, He works with tender care, causing no more pain than needed to smooth our coat. And God seeks to guide us in grooming each other, with His Spirit's still, small voice. Had I sought His counsel that day, instead of plunging ahead on my own, I'd have spared myself and Kate some needless hurt.

Biscuit's coat will form tangles as long as she lives. It's the nature of her fur. It's the nature of our flesh to form spiritual tangles. But God can remove them and teach us to groom as He does. If we follow His tender, loving lead, we're more likely to heal hearts, not nip them. And one day we will hear Him say, "Well done, good and faithful groomer."

If we confess our sins, he is faithful and just and will forgive us our sins and purify us from all unrighteousness (1 John 1:9).

Consider This

Do you have any spiritual mats that need combing out? If so, how might God want to do this? How might grooming now avoid worse tangles later?

How might you speak with blunted edges when grooming someone else?

A Tick in Time
Have You Picked Up Any "Ticks" in This Life?

*It's not a problem that we have
a problem. It's a problem if we
don't deal with the problem.*

MARY KAY UTECH

After hiking with me in the mountains, Gracie would occasionally return with a tick or two embedded in her skin. I'd discover them when I'd see her doing a contortionist act, twisting her body into a pretzel to bite out the irritating little pest. When it was impossible for her to reach the affected area with her teeth, she'd resort to scratching with her hind paw, which was a futile exercise.

I thought about how much easier it would be if she had hands. She could pour some olive oil on the tick to loosen it up a bit and then grab a pair of tweezers to pull it out. Oh, yes, and she'd also need a human brain to formulate and carry out the plan.

But I knew Gracie would never grow hands or get a job to earn the money to buy olive oil and tweezers or have the intelligence to figure out how to use these items.

So I'd step in with my higher-than-dog IQ and ten fingers. I'd tell Gracie to sit calmly so I could remove the tick. Too often, she'd squirm and snap, resisting my efforts. I'd have to pin her down or have someone else hold her steady so I could fix her problem in a quick and efficient way—totally outside the comprehension of a dog's mind. After a little oil and a small tug of the tweezers, Gracie would be off, tick free and happy.

It was fear of the unknown, of my non-dog methods, that made Gracie anxious. It was being afraid that I would hurt her in my efforts to remove the tick. I wonder how often I exhibit the same trepidation when God graciously wants to fix a problem in my life with means beyond my comprehension.

We all pick up "ticks" by living in this world—people or things that attach themselves to us and suck our energy, joy, and lifeblood. Often, because of emotional or spiritual attachments, we find it impossible to remove these people or things, even when God wants us to. We may know they are unhealthy for us, that we'd be better off without them, but no matter how much we contort ourselves, we can't shake them off. We try to use familiar methods, like Gracie scratching with her hind foot, but like Gracie, we only succeed in making the ticks dig in deeper.

I had a "friend" who was such a person. He was the kind of peer who made it easy for me to experience the crazier side of life. Many of the places we went and the characters we met were exciting and colorful—but not conducive to a closer walk with God. Other pals let me know they thought his friendship was more negative than positive. God let me know too. But in my limited human perspective, I found him difficult to remove.

At the time, I was seeking God—to clean up my act; to get on the straight path; to get emotionally, physically, and spiritually healthy. I prayed about this controversial friendship that was lodged under my skin. "Lord, please give me wisdom about how to deal with this guy. We have a lot of fun together—but I don't see all that much good fruit growing from our association. What am I supposed to do?"

Then I lent him something of value. We set a deadline for him to give it back. The deadline came and went. I waited and waited.

When I finally called and asked about it, he not only didn't return it, he made comments that hurt in a "bite the hand that feeds you" kind of way.

After I hung up the phone, I had an epiphany. This relationship was over. I can't explain it, but I felt all ties severed cleanly—like a tick plucked intact out of Gracie. After this call, I never heard from him again, and I felt no need to call him, either. In the same way that Gracie could not have come up with the oil, tweezers, and intelligence to remove her tick, I could not have come up with the circumstances that God orchestrated to remove this person from my life in the space of a short phone call.

Gracie felt a momentary pain when the tick was yanked out, followed by a far greater relief. It was the same for me. After God performed His operation and the hurt was no more, I harbored no bitterness or regret. With hindsight, I only saw God's careful hand in this, and I moved on with my life in positive ways.

God doesn't always remove our problems. But whether He does or not, He is infinitely wiser than we are in dealing with them. If we would submit to our Great Physician's loving care and healing touch, we might be pleasantly surprised at the results.

Trust in the Lord with all your heart, and do not rely on your own insight (Proverbs 3:5 NRSV).

Consider This

Is there a person or problem in your life that has you at your wits' end? How has your own insight failed you? Are you willing to give it to God, or are you afraid to do so? If you're afraid, what is it you fear might happen?

Habitude Adjustment
God's Word Works Change

One habit overcomes another.

Thomas à Kempis

All dogs lick, but Biscuit did it to excess. I used to call her Biscuit Busy Tongue. She was quick to swing into action, and she did it with gusto. If she saw I was crying, she pounced on me and scrubbed my face. It's as if she thought she could wash away my hurt. She also licked me as a morning greeting, or to lap salt or water from my skin. She could be quite persistent, and she didn't always stop when I asked her.

In time, I grew tired of being her salt lick or human lollipop. I decided Biscuit needed habitude adjustment. My strategy was simple. I would find a way to block her behavior. I thought about what would prevent her licking and taught her the command "head down." It worked. My dog could not lick with her chin on the floor.

Of course, my method had a major flaw. It halted Biscuit's tongue in its tracks, but it didn't address what caused the unwanted behavior. This meant if her chin came up, she might start to lick again. If the unwanted habit were a weed, I'd have chopped off the leaves, but left the roots, so it could sprout once more.

My Master has a far better way to do habitude adjustment on me. He treats the habit at its source with a skillful application of His Word. He is doing this with my habit of doubting myself with respect to my writing.

I was born into a family that places high value on human achievement. My self-esteem is wrapped up in my work—too much. And if I'm honest, my pride is also involved. I want to look good to others. And so I get hung up and paralyzed by my fear of failure. If I get stuck on something I'm writing, I get down on myself, the dragon of self-doubt rears its ugly head, and I want to flee instead of pushing through.

Some time ago, a close friend suggested I let God's Word start to work on this problem. She knew I was struggling to complete a book series. "Ask God to give you a verse for the project. Then put it up near your computer. Read it every day before you start working," she counseled.

I prayed. God pointed me to a verse in the book of Joshua: "Have I not commanded you? Be strong and courageous. Do not be terrified; do not be discouraged, for the LORD your God will be with you wherever you go" (Joshua 1:9).

I posted the verse. I read it each day. It's not an instant fix, but it keeps reminding me that my success depends on God's adequacy, not my own. It's not about believing in me; it's about believing in Him. If He's called me to the task, He will walk beside me in it.

Just as this one verse gives me God's perspective, so does all of Scripture. There is one overarching habit which can help adjust all others. This habit is regular, consistent Bible study. For many years, I'd failed to develop this discipline in my life. And then, during one of my drought times, God acted to change things.

At a friend's invitation, I joined her Bible class. It was part of a nationwide program designed to help people study God's Word. The class met once a week. There was small-group discussion. There was a lecture. There was homework and a special written commentary. I was digging into Scripture every week. And over time, God's living Word did a habitude adjustment, working on me from the inside out. It changed my habit of looking at life from a human point of view. It got me used to seeing things through "God-colored glasses." That shift in focus has helped counteract the vertigo moments in life and given me an anchor nothing else could.

I'm still doing habitude adjustment with Biscuit, as my Master is with me. It isn't instant or easy. But God is faithful to complete the task. His Spirit will apply His Word to root out my hindering habits like weeds and plant His godly ones in their place, so one day I can stand before Him, fully sanctified in Christ.

For it is God who works in you to will and to act according to his good purpose (Philippians 2:13).

Consider This

Is there a habit you're struggling with, that you feel is holding you back? What might have caused it? What makes it hard to break? What Scriptures might you memorize and meditate on to help do habitude adjustment in this area?

Mine!

Don't Growl; Trust

*Nothing is enough to the man for
whom enough is too little.*

EPICURUS

The dogs were gobbling dinner, and Biscuit emptied her food bowl first. Her head inched toward Morgan's dish. He was having none of it.

"Grrrr!" he rumbled. "Mine!"

"Morgan, no growling!" I chided. But he'd do it again, I knew. Even after all this time, he wasn't always sure he'd get enough.

Morgan's first two years of life are a mystery to me. He was plucked from a shelter by a pet rescue group, and then I adopted him just days later. He was scrawny and fearful. If he felt cornered, he could turn aggressive. And if Biscuit or one of my cats vied for his food, a toy he wanted, or my lap, he would growl a warning. "Mine!"

I guessed that Morgan might have been on the streets, starved for food and love, forced to fend for himself. To survive, he had learned to protect what was his by growling. Now he had a new master who would gladly meet all his needs…but he didn't know that yet. So I showered him with love and good things, and gently tried to break the habit. Time passed. The growling lessened, but it didn't stop completely. I let it go. It had done no real harm.

And then, one day, it did.

I had taken the dogs on a visit to my mother's. While dinner was being prepared, a small piece of turkey fell on the kitchen floor. Morgan and my mom's dog, Pixie, dove for it together. Growls rang out and then a yelp of pain. It was over in a moment, but Pixie had been slightly injured.

I was horrified. How could my normally sweet little dog hurt poor Pixie over an insignificant scrap of turkey?

But I've done similar things. Like the time I didn't tell Grusha about the party.

I was working for my uncle as a writer at his small health charity. Grusha was my colleague, friend, and mother figure. She was also a "life of the party" type, and I wasn't. One day, my uncle invited me to a little function at his nearby business. He didn't specifically tell me to let Grusha know about it, but deep in my heart I knew she was included. Still, a part of me, some ugly insecure part, wanted this just for myself. I wanted to be special. So I said nothing, while my silence screamed out, "MINE!"

"Where's Grusha?" they asked at the party. Guilt washed over me as I mumbled some nonanswer. Back at home, I cried so hard I gave myself a monster headache. Grusha learned about it the next workday. She gazed at me with wounded wisdom. She realized I hadn't wanted her there. She pinpointed why…my insecurities, my fear that I wasn't enough. Then…she forgave me.

God could have said "Mine" when it came to His Son. He could have shouted it out when Jesus sweated blood in Gethsemane and pleaded that, if possible, the cup of His death be removed. But God so loved us that He gave what was His so our need for redemption could be met.

Our Master is still meeting our needs. We don't have to growl. His provision will not fail.

He who did not spare his own Son, but gave him up for us all—how will he not also, along with him, graciously give us all things? (Romans 8:32).

Consider This

What are the most important needs in your life right now? Which of these do you find it hardest to trust God for? Why is that?

Have you ever growled at or hurt another in an effort to get your needs met? What was the result?

Don't Fence Me Out
God Wants Us to Build Bridges, Not Walls

*It is never too late to give
up your prejudices.*

Henry David Thoreau

We got Max from a pet store. He'd been returned once because of a small birth defect. We didn't care about it. We thought he'd be a great dog. We took him home, and in no time at all, he settled in. He learned where his food and water were, and he found his own special spot to sleep. This was his home. He loved it. He loved us. He was comfortable and happy.

This went on for three years...until Kitty came.

We adopted Kitty from a kitten rescue organization. She, too, found her special places in our home and got comfortable. But Max was getting *uncomfortable*. This strange creature of a different breed was intruding on his space. Things were changing, and he didn't like it. Kitty caught his drift. Before long both Max and Kitty had a problem, and their problem was each other.

Max and Kitty started fighting like...well, like cats and dogs. Max chased Kitty all over the house. She fled from him till her fear and frustration were overcome by anger. Then she turned and became the aggressor, chasing while he ran from her. They went at it several times a day.

It was obvious they were horribly upset with one another. We thought of kicking one of them out of the house, but we hated to do that. We thought we'd wait a bit and see what happened.

Finally, we noticed something changing between Max and Kitty. They still chased each other, but they didn't seem angry now. Instead of trying to hurt each other, it seemed more as though they were playing a game. We figured they were tired of being at odds and would try to get along. This proved true. They still fought occasionally (just like people do), but most of the time they lived together in peace—much to our relief.

Like Max, I've recently felt invaded by a new breed in our neighborhood. And I must confess, I've struggled with it too.

I'm a farmer's wife. I've loved the farming community where we've lived. For nearly three decades, I've watched men and machinery prepare the ground for planting. I've watched crops grow from seed to harvest. I've seen the fields covered in cotton, wheat, alfalfa, and other produce that fed or clothed our nation and the world.

I've watched my children watch the fields. I've shared the bounty of our crops with our neighbors, and they've shared their bounty with us. That's what farming neighbors do.

Things change. Lives change. The lands change.

Developers are buying up the fields. They're chopping them up and building big new homes. These new neighborhoods are walled off with concrete fences.

Just like Max, I had my place and I was comfortable. Now that's changed, and I don't like it. I don't like that the concrete walls are destroying the view. To me, the walls symbolize distrust. I've heard their purpose is to keep the homeowners from being robbed, but I wish the countryside was open, as it used to be.

Just like Max, I'm also wary of my new breed of neighbors. Will they be city folk? Will they have fancy cars and clothes? Will I feel pressure to keep up with them, to do what city folk do?

My new neighbors have their issues too. They've complained about the farmers' dust. And they're worried about the chemicals we spray on the crops. But a farmer reports and gets permission for all the chemicals he uses. And how can you farm without making some dust now and then?

As I've thought of these things, I've recalled how Max and Kitty had a problem with each other. I've recalled how I, their master, wished that they could live in peace. And I've wondered, "What does my Master want of me?"

I've fussed about my new neighbors' concrete fences. But maybe it's my own inner walls that need knocking down. Maybe I'm the one with the fences of fear and distrust. Maybe I need to reach out and be the good neighbor God wants me to be. Even if they don't have crops to share, I could share the bounty of my crops with them. I could teach them the joys of country living. I could share my love, my heart, my life…my Lord.

The Jews and Samaritans of Jesus' day had a deep distrust and dislike of each other. But Jesus, a Jew, reached out to a Samaritan—the woman at the well. She brought her whole town to Him, and His love broke down their walls of distrust. They welcomed Him, and believed on Him as their Messiah.

God wants me to reach out in love to those who are different too…and live in peace with them, the way Max and Kitty did.

Love does no harm to its neighbor. Therefore, love is the fulfillment of the law (Romans 13:10).

Consider This

Have you built walls of fear and distrust in your life? What has caused this? Are you willing to knock them down? How can you begin to do so?

See Stuart Run

Are You Using Your Gifts for God's Glory?

Hide not your Talents, they for Use were made.
What's a Sun-Dial in the Shade!

BENJAMIN FRANKLIN

God gave Stuart four strong legs, a quick mind, and a loud bark. We knew these gifts and talents would make Stuart a great watchdog some day. But when he was a puppy, he preferred to use them to chase cats.

We lived on a farm surrounded by acres of almond trees. For us, that meant having multiple cats around. Stuart seemed to think these felines existed solely for his entertainment. He never hurt them; he just loved to annoy them. They didn't think it was nearly as much fun as he did.

At Stuart's approach, some cats would run, which spurred him to race after them as fast as his puppy legs could go. Others took up a battle stance, fur standing on end. One brave mama cat, if pressed, would pounce, her claws digging into Stuart's thick fur. He retreated, humiliated…but only until the pain wore off. Then it was back to the fray again.

Stuart would often chase some poor cat from the front porch clear out to the orchard, where most likely it would climb a tree. He'd stand sentry below, barking till he tormented not only every feline within earshot, but the humans as well. Sometimes he'd get so caught up in the moment he'd climb the tree himself. When he realized he was in a place where dogs didn't belong, he would carefully climb down again and launch into his meaningless woofing once more.

Stuart played like a puppy. He spoke like a puppy. But his woofing wouldn't always be pointless noise. As he matured, he began to bark at strangers and chase unwanted critters from our yard. More and more, he used his talents to please me, his master.

God gives us gifts and talents too. When we're immature, like Stuart was, we may use them more to please ourselves than our Lord. When I was a "puppy," I did that with my musical abilities. I started singing on stage at age four, and took up clarinet in fourth grade. In high school, I played the little B♭ clarinet during marching season. But I played the biggest clarinet, the contrabass, during concert season so I could try out for county honor band. My goal freshman year was to get out of school for rehearsals...and I achieved it.

Sophomore year saw my objective shift to chasing boys—actually, one in particular. He sat first chair trumpet and went to another school. Band practice was a great way to see him. Happily, I had better luck than Stuart had with cats.

Still, my Master, who had given me my musical gifts, had so much more in mind. Time passed. I graduated and grew up. As my relationship with my heavenly Father matured, His desires became mine. I longed to use music not just for my own enjoyment but to serve my Lord. I sang on the worship team at church. I helped start a community band. When my children were in elementary school, I wrote and directed the school Christmas programs. I taught classroom music to children, and we sang songs about God and country. As I've used my gifts for God, He has multiplied them in the lives of others.

He has given me unexpected blessings as well—bands I played in were privileged to perform for two presidents, Ford and Reagan, when they visited our city. Oh, and remember the first chair trumpet player in honor band? I married him!

When I was a "puppy" like Stuart, I never dreamed what God might do with the gifts He had given me. Puppies don't think in those terms, but God does. If we let Him mature us and seek to please Him, He will bless our gifts and multiply our joy.

When I was a child, I talked like a child, I thought like a child, I reasoned like a child. When I became a man, I put childish ways behind me (1 Corinthians 13:11).

Consider This

What gifts and talents do you believe God has given you? How can you use them to glorify Him and bless and encourage others?

Catch as Catch Can't

Do You Need a Reality Check?

*The house of delusions is cheap
to build but drafty to live in.*

A.E. HOUSMAN

When Gracie and I hiked in the mountains behind our house, we occasionally encountered a deer. Upon spotting this swift-of-foot creature, Gracie would assume a stalking position and creep up on her prey. When she calculated in her big-game-hunter mind that the deer was in striking distance, she would take off like a cheetah—and the chase was on.

Gracie was low-slung with stubby legs, yet she would run her heart out in hopes of catching one of these Olympic animal sprinters. She would kick up a cloud of dust as she chased a deer off the trail and then bound into the brush after it. As the deer would gracefully leap away with its long and powerful legs, Gracie would vanish in the undergrowth. Moments later she'd emerge, no deer in tow, but tail wagging proudly as if to say she could have caught that animal—but chose to let it go this time. Like an average Joe who dreams of marrying a supermodel, Gracie's dream of catching a deer was total fantasy.

Even though Gracie took her hunting seriously, from my point of view, her quest was silly from the get-go. There was no way my rotund little mutt could catch a deer. But as Gracie's master, I decided these chases were harmless for both parties. The deer never got caught, and Gracie always gave up before she collapsed with a heart attack. I suppose that if she had managed to snag her prey by some weird twist of fate, I'd have had to intervene. The deer probably could have done more harm to her than she could have done to it. But in her whole life, this was never to be the case.

Sometimes, chasing fantasies has bigger, longer-range implications, like Don Quixote chasing windmills, or like me, as a single guy, chasing the girl of my dreams.

For many years, I pursued an ideal image in my mind and heart—the perfect Proverbs 31 woman who would complete my life and look great doing it. She'd be an incredible combination of brains, beauty, and godly virtues. She'd speak multiple languages, have a wonderful sense of humor, and hold down a good job with health benefits in case my career didn't take off. And most importantly, after I'd found this perfect woman, she'd have to have one last essential quality to make it a done deal—she'd somehow have to find me attractive and perfect too.

This, of course, was an utter impossibility. But hey, I didn't let that keep me from the hunt. I spent thousands of hours and dollars in pursuit of something I could never catch. (Gracie chasing a deer doesn't seem so silly when I think about this.)

It was a twofold problem: 1) My dream girl was a fantasy and no real woman could live up to my expectations, and 2) If my dream girl did exist, I would not be her dream guy. Even though all logic told me to be still and seek God in this matter, I'd rush head over heels after my fantasies while they bounded away gracefully up the side of a steep mountain. I'd try my best to fight through the underbrush and hold on to the rocks—but eventually, I'd tumble down and be back where I started. I'd emerge from the shrubs, scratched and bruised, and tell my pals I could have caught that girl—but when I got up close, she was less than perfect, so I had to let her go. Besides, there were a lot more deer in the forest.

My friends called this behavior the James Bond syndrome. We grew up watching the most beautiful, intelligent, and sexy women—who also had tenth-degree black belts in karate and multiple PhDs—literally throw themselves at 007 with his well-timed wink. This was how it was supposed to be. This was how men and women hooked up in relationship. You believed you were Bond trapped inside an average body, and all you had to do was smile at that supermodel rocket scientist and she'd follow you anywhere.

Looking back, I wonder how my Father in heaven viewed my pursuit of the perfect Eve. I wonder if He felt the same way I did watching Gracie chase deer.

Gracie's perfect day would have been for her to catch that deer, bring it down, and drag it triumphantly out of the woods. That's what motivated her to pursue the animal in the first place. But I, being a bit wiser than my pup, knew that this perfect deer scenario only existed in the forest of Gracie's mind. However, since she only chased her fantasy for a few minutes a month, I, her master, saw it as more fun than harm.

I'm sure my Master took a different view as He watched me spend half my life chasing a perfect woman who existed only in my mind. Did He see it as healthy or productive? Was it His plan? I think not.

Finally, I learned to see my life from God's perspective. When I did, I realized I was chasing a fantasy I could never catch. I was just like Gracie—a chunky little dog trying to chase down a deer. But unlike Gracie, my deer didn't even exist, and I was spending not minutes but years in pursuit of a mirage. It wasn't until I realized that I was less than perfect that I could finally settle down and allow God to bless me with my perfect match—a less-than-perfect woman.

As I look back on my single life, I remember having a lot of fun. But as the years passed, and after each failed relationship ended, I had an uneasy feeling inside that what I was doing was not healthy.

Now that I have a wife and son, I'm very thankful to God that He stepped in to dissolve my delusions, free me with His truth, and give me the real woman of my dreams.

> *The* Lord *is righteous in all his ways and loving toward all he has made. The* Lord *is near to all who call on him, to all who call on him in truth. He fulfills the desires of those who fear him (Psalm 145:17-19).*

Consider This

Have you chased any fantasies in your life? Do you think they were harmless or problematic? Have you let them go? If so, what has taken their place?

Mount Saint Morgan
God Meets Us Where We Are

*It is with our passions as it is
with fire and water; they are good
servants, but bad masters.*

Sir Roger L'Estrange

Perhaps you have heard of Mount Saint Helens, a peak in Washington's Cascade Range famous for its volcanic eruptions. Well, my dog Morgan has a history of eruptions too. The first time I saw him go off was shortly after I'd adopted him. We were in the car. I stopped to get gas. The attendant began to wash my windshield. Suddenly, Morgan lunged at the glass, barking furiously. Luckily, my car's doors and windows were closed, and all he could do was woof. It shocked me. I had never seen this "Mount Saint Morgan" aspect of my dog.

I saw it often in the next weeks and months. I soon realized that Morgan's fear was boiling over like lava. He'd been rescued from a shelter, and he'd clearly had some trauma in his past life. From what I could see, loud sounds and strangers were most apt to set him off. I couldn't get inside his head, so I didn't always know when he might blow. At times, he'd appear to be fine with folks—then launch into a barking fit without warning—scaring them and me. I countered this by cautioning guests about Morgan's hang-ups so they would be prepared in case he went off.

I loved Morgan dearly. I met him where he was, determined to help him heal. In time, he began to improve. But he could still erupt now and then. Once, a friend brought her son over, and I failed to keep track of the dog and the child. Suddenly, I heard terrified screams and woofing. I raced upstairs. The child was pressed against the wall, howling, while Morgan barked frantically at him. It turned out the boy had a prior fear of pooches. I think they scared each other. Happily, no harm was done, and in later years they met again under friendlier circumstances. But even today, after I, his master, have worked with him for seven years, Morgan still erupts sometimes.

After nearly 40 years with my Master, I still erupt at times too.

Even as a child, I had a more volatile temperament than some. My most common triggers were stress and frustration. When my heavenly Master rescued me, He was fully aware of this Mount Saint Marion aspect of His child. But He loved me dearly and knew He could transform me with His love. He set to work on me, just as I did with Morgan.

Over time, God has shown me that, like my dog, I am apt to blow when fear bubbles over. I dread failure, and I erupt when my feelings of inadequacy build. I'm angry, but the anger stems from feeling bad about myself. I still recall a stint as a writer on a particular live action kids' TV show. It wasn't a good fit. I wasn't cutting it, and I knew it. One evening, around midnight, all alone in my home office, my pain bubbled over. I screamed at the four walls and railed at God. "Why did You let me take this assignment if You knew I would fail?" I howled. Only later could I see and accept that He had used the setback to build my character, and that was far more important than momentary career success.

As I have matured in my walk with God, He has built my faith in Him. He has shown me that my self-esteem must be grounded in His love, not my human achievements. He has also taught me to share my foibles honestly with others. I've warned friends that I can erupt under pressure, asked their forgiveness in advance, and begged them not to take it personally if I lose control. That doesn't give me permission to sin, but it gives them perspective when I stumble in my humanness. And these cautions can be protective... just like my warnings about Morgan.

I'd like to think that my eruptive tendencies have lessened over the years, just like Morgan's have. Alas, at times I wonder. In the middle of a deadline on this very book, my brand-new desktop computer crashed. I did a Mount Saint Marion routine when I dialed tech support. My behavior fell far short of God's standards.

But perhaps I can glean some encouragement from another recent incident. A few days ago I went out through the garage to get my morning paper. My housemate was leaving for work at that moment. Her job had been stressful, she was low on rest, and her brain was on autopilot. As she drove away, she pressed her garage door opener. The door descended—locking me out.

I stared in horror as her car disappeared down the street. I hadn't memorized her cell phone number. I had no idea if my neighbors were home. Even if they were, I didn't relish knocking on their door. I was in my pajamas—decent, but not what you'd call presentable. But I had to get to a phone. My housemate planned to be gone all day. If I couldn't reach her, I'd be locked out all that time, in this getup...as my manuscript ticked down to deadline. Yikes!

The lava bubbled. Panic swelled inside me. Even as it did so, I cried out to God. Mercifully, the neighbors were there. They lent me their phone. I reached a friend who had my housemate's number, and I got her on the line. Even though I sputtered as I spoke with her, I was agitated rather than angry. I knew that if I'd been stressed and tired, I could easily have done what she had. When she returned, I was quick to assure her I wasn't upset with her. Indeed, in short order I was laughing about the episode and plotting how I could use it in this very story. And I give my Master all the credit.

I also give Christ all the credit for not erupting when He had every right to: when He was seized unjustly, tried, tortured, and hung on a cross between a pair of thieves. But my Savior kept His cool and died to pay for me losing mine. He took care of Mount Saint Marion on Mount Calvary. I pray that next time I'm tempted to blow, I'll recall His example, and follow it more closely.

Make every effort to add to your faith goodness; and to goodness, knowledge; and to knowledge, self-control; and to self-control, perseverance; and to perseverance, godliness; and to godliness, brotherly kindness; and to brotherly kindness, love. For if you possess these qualities in increasing measure, they will keep you from being ineffective and unproductive in your knowledge of our Lord Jesus Christ (2 Peter 1:5-9).

Consider This

What situations or comments are most likely to make you blow? What underlying causes might be behind these eruptions? How do they impact those around you? What biblical truths or promises might help prevent them?

How a Dog Became a Butterfly
God Frees Us from Old Baggage

*Where there is great love, there
are always miracles.*

WILLA CATHER

When I first met Morgan, he was a shivering lump of black-and-tan fur. I'd been looking for a rescue dog, and his face caught my eye. A volunteer set him on my lap. As I cuddled him, I fell in love and adopted him on the spot.

It didn't take long to learn that my little guy came with some baggage. I've already written of how he spooked at loud sounds and strangers. His baggage also came out with me, though in a different way. We had formed a bond. He trusted me. But if I showed any displeasure with him, he cowered, tucking his tail. The fear he showed went far beyond the norm, and it tore at my heart.

I'd adopted Morgan. He had a new life. But the vestiges of his old life clung to him. It's as if he'd been a caterpillar and become a butterfly. But his old cocoon of fear stuck to his wings and bound him so he couldn't take flight. I felt my love could free him. I tried to make him feel safe and adored. When he became a little more secure, I worked to lessen his negative responses to others. He seemed to cower a little less, to be just a bit more outgoing. He was learning to expect good things from people, not bad. Morgan's transformation took time, but slowly, he began to fly.

Thinking of Morgan makes me recall how I started my new life in Christ, in my junior year of college. I, too, was adopted…by my heavenly Master. I, too, came with a pile of baggage. Though I had become a new creation, old experiences and past hurts still clung to me. This sticky cocoon held me back. Part of that cocoon was a fear of rejection.

My cocoon got stickier my senior year. Problems with a Christian roommate made me feel like a failure. Christmas break was a downer. My parents didn't share my faith. I had no siblings. I had no church to turn to. My isolation deepened. Dark clouds of depression hung over me. It was then my Master sent His healing love from a totally unexpected source.

I had gone to a shopping center near home. Spying an ice-cream store, I went in to drown my sorrows in sweets. I found out that the woman scooping ice cream also knew the Lord. We started talking. She'd been going through some tough times in her own life, but this amazing lady was standing firm in Christ. She knew her Bible. She saw my need. And over the next two weeks, that wonderful child of God became my wing cleaner. She quoted to me from Scripture. She scrubbed at my fears and doubts with her faith and her love. And when I returned to school, my spiritual wings were just a bit lighter, though I must admit I'd spooned some ice-cream weight on my physical body.

That was nearly 40 years ago. I never saw the ice-cream lady again. But my Master has stayed by my side and continued to love me. And He has kept on cleaning my wings through His Word, His Spirit, and my fellow believers, just as I keep cleaning Morgan's, so we can be freed to fly like butterflies were meant to.

As I write this, I'm reminded of one more thing. Morgan is a mix. A friend once suggested he might have some papillon in him. The word "papillon" is French and refers to the breed's distinctive ears. It means butterfly.

Therefore, if anyone is in Christ, he is a new creation; the old has gone, the new has come! (2 Corinthians 5:17).

Consider This

Do you have old baggage clinging to you that makes it hard to fly in Christ? How does it hinder you? Have you asked God to clean your wings, directly or through others?

How might you be a wing cleaner for God and encourage someone else?

Doggie See, Doggie Do
Beware of the Company You Keep

*Tell me thy company, and I'll
tell thee what thou art.*

Miguel de Cervantes

Gracie was an only dog and rarely got into serious mischief, but when her best pal, Lucy the Border Collie, came for extended visits, anything was possible. Not that Lucy was a bad dog, but the combination of them being together, with a lot of idle time, brought out the animal in them.

I recall one particular time when Lucy was staying for the week. Typically, she and Gracie would romp and wrestle nonstop until they wore themselves out and napped. One morning I left and came back a few hours later to discover some intrigue in the backyard. It was around Halloween, and I found a whole pumpkin, about the size of a volleyball, lying innocuously on the ground. There were suspicious teeth marks in it. This pumpkin had not been in the backyard when I left.

I was amazed, in the way we modern folk wonder how the Egyptians built the Great Pyramid. How did these mere dogs lift a smooth, round pumpkin without the use of hands and carry it into my backyard? It must've weighed about ten pounds, heavy for a medium-sized dog to carry in its mouth. And how did they get it through the fence? My backyard is rather jungle-like and there may be a few gaps here and there in the fencing, but it would take a detective to find them—or two dogs sniffing around for a few hours with nothing better to do.

As for the physical heist of the pumpkin, I wish I'd had a surveillance camera set up. I'm sure the footage would have been priceless, worthy of a "silliest dog home video" TV show. I can imagine Gracie and Lucy biting into the pumpkin, side by side, and carrying it together; or both of them pushing the big orange ball with their noses, shoving it through a secret hole in the fence.

What I wonder most about the pumpkin theft is...why? I could understand stealing bones, plush toys, a sheepskin bed, or a rawhide chew—but a pumpkin? The mystery got to be such an aggravating mind game I even asked the dogs, "How and why did you guys do this?" I half expected a reply, but their only response was silly-looking dog grins—like foreigners who pretend not to speak English when you're hopelessly trying to communicate in their native tongue.

Years later, when I muse on this incident, what lingers is that Gracie would *never* have done this on her own. It was beyond her solo capacity for mischief. I believe the same about Lucy. Trespassing on a neighbor's property and stealing that pumpkin was a two-dog inspiration. While amusing and somewhat harmless (no neighbors ever complained), this dubious doggie deed could have had more harmful consequences if the object stolen was of more value or of a more dangerous nature.

As in the case of these canines, the people we choose as our human companions can influence our actions, both for good and for bad.

Proverbs 13:20 tells us that "he who walks with the wise grows wise, but a companion of fools suffers harm."

When I thought about how peer pressure got me into trouble, an old memory popped into my head. I was five or six years old and hanging out with my brother, my sister, and my pal Mike. Mike was an adventurous kid who always pushed the envelope, enticing us to explore musty old basements, to climb dangerous trees, to throw rocks at things we shouldn't be throwing rocks at. One day our little gang came across a corral with a few horses in it. Mike dared me to crawl inside. I was certainly scared and would never have thought to do this on my own. But at his goading, I did.

The next thing I knew, I was being kicked around in the dirt by the horse. I think I spun around a few times, but, fortunately, I escaped serious harm. (Now that I have a small boy of my own, I realize how flexible kids' bodies are.) Needless to say, I am very thankful to be writing this today with my brains still intact and functioning. I think this illustrates how "a companion of fools suffers harm."

But the opposite is true when we choose wise companions. Hebrews 10:24-25 says, "Let us consider how we may spur one another on toward love and good deeds. Let us not give up meeting together, as some are in the habit of doing, but let us encourage one another."

One day, after church, a friend and I were convicted about doing good deeds instead of merely talking about them. We decided to go to a nearby nursing home and visit the elderly tenants. This was out of my comfort zone. To randomly choose a nursing home and drop in like a door-to-door salesman was something I'd never do on my own. And I know my friend wouldn't have gone on her own, either. Like Gracie and Lucy, we were made bolder by being two instead of one.

We prayed and then walked onto the nursing home property and both felt God lead us to a woman who seemed as though she was waiting for us to visit. She was sitting out in the parking lot in her wheelchair, happily smoking a cigarette. We struck up a conversation and found out she was a Christian. Her name was Gertrude, and to make a long story short, I wound up visiting her almost every week after church for years. Some days it would turn into a party, with four, five, or six others joining me to visit Gertrude. She was a cancer survivor, and even though cigarettes were not what the doctor ordered, smoking was one of the few things that gave her pleasure. We'd push her out on the sidewalk where she'd puff away at her precious cigarettes. We'd laugh, tell stories, and pray. Someone gave her a haircut. We exchanged gifts. Gertrude wound up giving us nicknames. Mine was "Tadpole." It was truly a blessed time that came about as the result of positive peer pressure, a beautiful illustration of how we each spurred one another toward love and good deeds that would not have come about on our own.

It absolutely matters who we choose to spend time with. Our companions can influence us for better or for worse.

Two dogs come together to steal a pumpkin.

A bunch of foolish kids goad one boy into getting kicked by a horse.

Fellow believers inspire each other to brighten up an old woman's life and discover that she blesses them as much as, if not more than, they bless her.

Imagine the possibilities when we choose to spend time with God.

Our fellowship is with the Father and with his Son, Jesus Christ (1 John 1:3).

Consider This

How have your peers influenced you—for better or for worse? How have you influenced them? How has spending time with God changed your life? What "good things" have you done because of your relationship with Christ that you couldn't have done alone?

All Hung Up
Had a Spiritual Checkup Lately?

*No one is more a slave than he who
thinks he is free without being so.*

GOETHE

One of Morgan's favorite spots to hide is under my bed, with only his plumed tail peeking from beneath its ruffled skirt. When I call he wriggles out nose first, bounding after me to the day's next adventure. This day was different. He didn't follow. He yelped in pain. I turned and saw to my shock that his paw was caught on his ear.

Morgan's a mix—sheltie with a few other things thrown in. The fur on his floppy ears is of varying lengths. The nail of one paw had caught on a strand of this fur, and he was all hung up. Of course, he had no idea what was wrong. All he knew was that he could barely move, and it hurt when he tried. I rushed to help. His panic and the paw's painful angle made him yelp yet again as I struggled to unhook him. But moments later, to both our relief, he was free and raced after me once more.

As I've reflected on Morgan's mishap, I've realized there are times when I get hung up, and it hinders me from following my Master. For years, my paw was caught on my ear in my relationship with my mother. She wanted to be close, especially after Dad died, but I pushed her away. My excuse was that our personalities were different. Never mind that God commands us to honor our parents. Resisting His prodding, I chose to see Mom less rather than more. I blamed her perfectionism and her need to be right. She blamed my insensitivity to her feelings and my lack of love.

Then, Mom got sick. Her blood pressure soared. She developed strange symptoms. She feared she might die. How we both dealt with this only heightened the tension between us.

A Christian friend pulled me aside. He urged me to get right with Mom and ask her forgiveness. He warned if I didn't and she passed away, it would haunt me.

I took the advice, but there was still a stumbling block between us. Things came to a head in a phone call. Mom and I had yet another difference of opinion. I hung up feeling negated. She called back and apologized, but the sting lingered. That afternoon, I was reading a classic of the Christian faith, *The Green Letters* by Miles J. Stanford. The text explained that at times we must come to the end of ourselves in order for God to work in a problem area of our lives. I felt I had come to the end of myself in my relationship with my mother. I knew I ought to love her. I now wanted to love her. But I feared I didn't, not really. What was wrong?

I prayed. And God showed me where I was hung up. I was looking to Mom for the affirmation and self-esteem that only He could give. This was catching my emotional paw on my ear in our relationship.

I'd actually known this for a very long time, but the pain of Mom's illness, the fresh wound of our earlier phone call, and the words of that book drove this truth through my heart in a new and deeper way. I was finally ready to surrender my will and love Mom as God commanded.

Tears stung my eyes as I told God I would look to Him and Him only to meet my need for self-worth. And I promised to love Mom unconditionally, no strings attached. God unhooked my paw. My relationship with Mom was transformed.

That was six years ago. Mom still has health problems, but they're being managed. Our relationship is thriving. I have basked in her approval. She has basked in my love. We're both grateful to God for giving us a second chance. Of course, we still have our moments, but they don't last. We talk them through. And if all else fails, I cry out to my Master, and He unhooks my paw.

Search me, O God, and know my heart; test me and know my anxious thoughts. See if there is any offensive way in me, and lead me in the way everlasting (Psalm 139:23-24).

Consider This

Is there an area of your life where you feel hindered from following God? Have you asked God to show you where you are hung up?

Is there someone you've struggled with that God is calling you to love unconditionally?

Part V

Master Knows Best

Blind Spots

Seek God's Discernment

A fool sees not the same tree
that a wise man sees.

William Blake

After a long hike in the mountains, Gracie was anxious to jump in the back of my old Toyota pickup and rest. As we approached the dirt parking lot, she ran ahead of me. There were rarely any other cars parked here on weekdays—but this day a new silver BMW sat beside my truck. Gracie's usual practice was to dart ahead and leap into my open tailgate where a bowl of cool water awaited. But not being automobile savvy, Gracie ran forth and leaped onto the trunk of the BMW instead.

I was shocked. After checking to make sure the BMW wasn't scratched (thank goodness), I found myself somewhat amused. I'd always thought of Gracie as smart and intuitive. She knew that when I turned off my computer and it *beeped,* it was time for a walk. Merely by hearing the sound of a car parking outside my house, she could differentiate between familiar vehicles and those of strangers. But this morning, as I watched her fling herself onto the highly waxed surface of that silver Beemer, mistaking it for my white Toyota pickup, I could only think, *Gracie doesn't see things the way I do. She can't discern between automobiles by sight.* (Note: If she had slid off the BMW and injured herself, this lack of discernment could have had more serious consequences than mere embarrassment.)

As a car enthusiast, I can tell the difference between the 1955 and 1956 Chevrolet Bel Airs by their front grill designs. I know that only the 1963 Corvette had the split rear window. I can discern a '65 Mustang from a '66 Mustang by their hubcaps. But Gracie couldn't even discern a new BMW from an old Toyota truck. To prevent her from making similar mistakes in the future, I would have had to mount big warning signs in dog language in front of all the other cars in the lot: NOT YOUR MASTER'S TRUCK—DO NOT JUMP IN!

I can discern different models of cars far better than Gracie the dog. But before I balloon with pride, I must consider that God can discern things I have trouble seeing. He has even put up warning signs in human language, in His Word, cautioning me to look more closely, lest I be deceived.

Matthew 7:15-16 warns, "Watch out for false prophets. They come to you in sheep's clothing, but inwardly they are ferocious wolves. By their fruit you will recognize them."

Though these verses are talking about false teachers, there are myriad examples of people being different on the inside than they seem on the outside. God sees the truth because He looks at the heart. I don't have His discernment. If I leap ahead, the way Gracie did, and don't ask Him for guidance, I may get into trouble. I may embrace a warm, fuzzy sheep, not knowing that inside, it is really a ferocious wolf.

I still recall one such incident. I was looking for someone to repair some vintage audio equipment. I had a fear of cold-calling, but after a few months of networking, I found a possible repairman. He claimed he was a Christian. My mind leaped ahead, jumping to the conclusion that this must be from God. I even paid him in cash, in advance, because he said he was in a jam. But he never finished the work he promised to do. I made numerous phone calls, but my messages were ignored. It's been years, and the matter has never been rectified.

This man talked the talk and wore the "Christian" label on his sheep's clothing, but his actions didn't match up with his outward appearance. I didn't find this out until too late. Sometimes I look at people the way Gracie looked at cars. I lack discernment.

But I could have asked God.

I'm sure God saw the wolf beneath the sheep costume when I hired this man. What if I had consulted with God before forking over my money? I might have avoided a painful mistake, just as Gracie might have avoided leaping onto that Beemer if she'd waited for my guidance.

The Bible tells us that Jesus knew the hearts and minds of those He encountered. In Mark 2:6-8 we read, "Some teachers of the law were sitting there, thinking to themselves, 'Why does this fellow talk like that? He's blaspheming! Who can forgive sins but God alone?' Immediately Jesus knew in his spirit that this was what they were thinking in their hearts, and he said to them, 'Why are you thinking these things?'"

This same mind-and-heart-reading Jesus lives within us today, if we have accepted Him as our Lord and Savior. We can ask Him to help us discern between good-for-us and not-so-good-for-us people. My mishap with the repairman only cost me a small sum of money, but lack of discernment may have far greater consequences. Whom should we marry? Whom should we choose as our business partners? Should we let this "nice" salesman into our house?

God sees the difference between sheep and wolves as clearly as we humans see the difference between a new BMW and a truck. No matter how righteous a sheep may look from our point of view, it's best to check with Him first. There may be a wolf hiding inside.

The LORD does not look at the things man looks at. Man looks at the outward appearance, but the LORD looks at the heart (1 Samuel 16:7).

Consider This

Have you ever been deceived by a wolf in sheep's clothing? How were you taken in? How might God, and His Word, help you better discern between sheep and wolves in the future?

Eyes to See, Ears to Hear

God Must Open Our Eyes to His Truth

The true seeing is within.

GEORGE ELIOT

Once in a while, a dog would appear on TV—doing something I wished Gracie could do, like race across a park, leap into the air, and catch a flying Frisbee in her mouth. I'd call Gracie out from under the dining table. "Look at the TV! Check out that Frisbee-catching dog!" I'd tell her. But Gracie's eyes would stick to my pointing finger, totally oblivious to the screen. Then the TV dog would bark and I'd nudge Gracie. "Hey, did you hear that? The TV dog is calling your name!" But she still didn't look or respond. While real dogs barking a half mile away would have perked up Gracie's ears, TV dogs barking in our living room didn't even seem to exist for her.

I began to experiment. When something came on TV I thought Gracie would enjoy, I'd lift her up and sit her smack-dab in front of the screen—to see the meowing cat or bowl of gravy-covered dog food. But Gracie might as well have been staring at a blank wall. For some reason, my dog didn't see or hear the same images and sounds coming from the TV that I did.

This reminds me of how I used to see and hear the Bible.

My parents weren't Christians, but they had one of those huge faux leather-bound King James Bibles the size of an L.A. phonebook. Where it came from I don't know, but it was perpetually dusty because to our family it was as relevant as a slide rule. I peeked into it as a kid, but I was freaked out by the gory medieval color prints of Jesus' crucifixion.

I went to church with a friend for a short season when I was in the fifth grade. Struggling to stay awake during the sermons, I'd look into the King James Bibles supplied on the back of the pew in front of me. My young eyes quickly spotting a "thee," a "thou," and a "ye" or two was enough to make me close the Good Book for the next decade or so. I couldn't understand what people saw in the Bible, how some folks said they could hear from God by reading His Word. To me, it was like staring at a blank wall—or maybe like how Gracie viewed TV.

Mark 8:17-18 says, "Do you still not see or understand? Are your hearts hardened? Do you have eyes but fail to see, and ears but fail to hear?" I had physical eyes and ears, but without the opening of the spiritual eyes and ears of my heart, the power and true meaning behind God's Word was beyond my understanding. As I observed Gracie, I knew she was seeing and hearing the TV in the same way I'd been reading the Bible. She was picking it up in a purely physical sense, but not in the higher ways intended by the creator of the TV program. It was visually and aurally "blah, blah, blah."

If, sometime in the distant future, science is ever able to transplant human brains into our dogs, perhaps they would be able to enjoy television with us. Their eyes and ears would be opened to all the high and mighty things we humans see and hear on TV. But until and unless that figment of my imagination comes to pass, dogs like Gracie will be unable to comprehend even the best reruns of *Lassie* or *Scooby-Doo*.

In my own life, it wasn't an operation, but the indwelling of the Holy Spirit that opened my eyes and ears to all the high, mighty, and living words of the Bible.

I recall one particular time when I saw and heard something special in God's Word. I had been wondering what to do about my floundering screenwriting career (a common theme throughout my adult life). I was very low and shared with my wife that maybe I should give up writing. Maybe we should sell everything we owned and become missionaries somewhere far from Hollywood, preferably in a land with no TV or movie theaters. We prayed for guidance and mercy. I asked God if He knew how lousy, disappointed, and frustrated I was feeling. *Please, God, what am I supposed to do?*

Then, in one of those quirky little moments I'm embarrassed to admit to, I felt prompted to flip open a Bible. I told myself the first Scripture that met my eye would be *the* answer.

Now, I know this kind of thing is usually regarded as ridiculously immature theology. Nonetheless, feeling ridiculously immature, I grabbed the nearest Bible on my shelf—a paperback King James New Testament in a generic lavender cover (picked up for a quarter at a garage sale). It was a far cry from that 50-pound Holy Bible in my parents' house—but it had the same message inside.

The Bible opened to Hebrews 4. My eyes zeroed in on verse 14: "Seeing then that we have a great high priest, that is passed into the heavens, Jesus the Son of God, let us hold fast our profession" (KJV).

Okay, that was pretty wild. "Hold fast our profession." I knew that this verse was actually referring to our profession of faith, but could this King James New Testament be telling me to hold fast to my "profession"—that is, *the job of screenwriting?* This phrasing is only in the King James Version—that once dusty, musty, scary book that sat neglected on my parents' bookshelf. I didn't normally read this version. Was God telling me it was okay to see a double meaning in the word "profession?" Or—was I just being somewhat nutty and reading things into this? Only God truly knows—but His message to me continued in verse 15: "For we have not an high priest which cannot be touched with the feeling of our infirmities; but was in all points tempted like as we are, yet without sin."

Now I was back on more traditional theological ground. This answered the other part of my prayer: *Does God know how I feel?* Yes, Jesus knows what it feels like to be struggling and weary. He even wanted to quit the *profession* to which He had been called—that is, Savior. In Matthew 26:39, He cried out, "O my Father, if it be possible, let this cup pass from me: nevertheless not as I will, but as thou wilt" (KJV).

This happened more than four years ago, and I'm still persevering with my writing. I'm holding on to my *profession*—in the face of much adversity and disappointment. I'm not famous. I'm not making millions or winning Academy Awards, but I feel I'm on the path God designed for me. I know this because of His Word—not primarily because of the quirky "hold fast your *profession*" kinds of things (even though I still think that was cool)—but because God's Spirit fills my heart and assures me through His enlightened Word that He *knows* what I'm going through.

Once the Holy Spirit opened the eyes and ears of my heart, the once-boring Bible that I likened to staring at a wall was now alive with words popping off the pages with truth and wisdom, words able to touch and guide every aspect of my life. Gracie never in her lifetime had her eyes and ears miraculously opened to experience the fullness of television—but I'm so thankful God opened my eyes and ears so I could miraculously experience Him...the Living Word.

One thing I do know. I was blind but now I see!
(John 9:25).

Consider This

How has the Holy Spirit opened your eyes and ears so you could perceive truth that was hidden from you before? In what areas of your life do you feel you may still be blind and deaf?

What's It Worth?

Do You Value What God Values?

Thirst teaches the value of water.

PROVERB

When I first got Gracie, I locked her in the kitchen so she wouldn't wander into the rest of the house and get into mischief. I put the trash can on top of the washing machine so she couldn't dig in it. I installed a doggie door so she could go outside whenever she wanted. I kept human food and drink and dangerous chemicals out of her reach.

But I didn't stash my library books.

One day I came home to find *The Day of the Jackal* chewed up. A few weeks later, it was another hard-hitting adventure novel, *Rising Sun*. Gracie couldn't read, and even if she could have, I don't think she'd have gravitated toward these kinds of action stories. The only value she found in them was to use them as expensive and short-lived chew toys to alleviate her boredom. I had to pay the library full price for these damaged books, and needless to say, I didn't leave any unattended fiction volumes around her again.

I didn't punish Gracie for destroying these books. I knew she couldn't understand the value of the printed word any more than I could understand the value of an old bone that she would fight to the death to keep.

Likewise, my four-year-old son doesn't always comprehend the worth of things. Recently, I tested him to gauge his understanding of the value of money. I held a 100-dollar bill in one hand—and two shiny pennies in the other. I asked Skye which he preferred. He shifted his gaze thoughtfully between the piece of paper and the two bright copper objects. He reached toward the bill, changed his mind, grabbed the two pennies, and went merrily on his way. He had no idea a piece of paper with a picture of a funny-looking long-haired man on it was equal to 10,000 shiny pennies.

His choice made me smile. I thought about Gracie and what choice she'd have made if I'd offered her similar options. If I'd held out a meatball in one hand and a diamond-studded Rolex watch in the other, she would have gobbled the beef any day. Neither Gracie nor Skye valued things the same way I did.

I've not always valued things the same way God does.

Recently a Christian friend dropped by unexpectedly on a Sunday. The past days had been an extremely busy time. I'd been in the midst of an incredibly demanding writing assignment that could have kept me busy eight days a week. But I took time to relax and fellowship with him for hours because of a choice I made a while ago. No matter how crazy it gets or what demands are placed on me as a screenwriter, I don't work on screenplays on the Sabbath day. In the eyes of the world, choosing Sabbath rest over lucrative work is choosing the two pennies over the hundred bucks. But in the eyes of God, the Sabbath has far greater value.

Isaiah 58:13-14 says, "If you keep your feet from breaking the Sabbath and from doing as you please on my holy day, if you call the Sabbath a delight and the LORD's holy day honorable, and if you honor it by not going your own way and not doing as you please or speaking idle words, then you will find your joy in the LORD."

Plainly speaking, if I keep the Sabbath, then I will find "joy in the Lord." And God promises in Psalm 37:4, "Delight yourself in the LORD and he will give you the desires of your heart."

Talk about a good deal. Talk about value. It should be a no-brainer for believers, like choosing between the two pennies and the 100-dollar bill. Will I place greater value on writing screenplays seven days a week to *potentially* earn a few bucks and a fleeting 15 minutes of fame? Or will I place greater worth on the Sabbath, rest from writing, delight myself in God, and put myself in a position for Him to give me the desires of my heart?

In past years I couldn't have cared less about keeping the Sabbath. I'd have put it in the same old-school category as wearing sackcloth and ashes. I wrote seven days a week because I highly valued success and the things that money could buy. I undervalued the Sabbath as much as Gracie undervalued library books or Skye undervalued Benjamin Franklin on a C-note.

However, as I grew in the Word, the value of the Sabbath grew accordingly. I began to look forward to pulling off from the weekly bumper-to-bumper rat race—and parking my weary soul at a "God stop" of spiritual and physical restoration. I began to see my Creator's wisdom in giving me a special day to simply be still and know Him better.

And if that's not enough to convince you of the Sabbath's value, don't forget it's number three on the Lord's all-time "Top Ten" list, the Ten Commandments.

Remember the Sabbath day by keeping it holy. Six days you shall labor and do all your work, but the seventh day is a Sabbath to the LORD your God. On it you shall not do any work....For in six days the LORD made the heavens and the earth, the

sea, and all that is in them, but he rested on the seventh day. Therefore the Lord blessed the Sabbath day and made it holy (Exodus 20:8-11).

Consider This

What things do you value most in life? Are they in line with what God values most? If not, why not?

What is keeping the Sabbath worth to you, and why?

Lost in Translation
God's Priorities Might Not Be Ours

Beyond all mystery is the mercy of God.

ABRAHAM JOSHUA HESCHEL

When I used to write on a laptop at the dining room table, Gracie loved to sit nearby. She'd curl up in a comfortable spot and watch me. Her interest wasn't in *what* I was writing, but in *when* I would *stop* writing. The glorious words that flowed out of my mind and onto the computer screen were utter gibberish to her.

Even though my work may have been worthy of great financial reward, this was of no concern to my dog. She'd yawn as my fingers banged out inspired prose, but she'd sit up with excitement when she saw me lean back and stretch—filling her with the hope that I would soon feed her or take her for a hike in the mountains. I may have been churning out a masterpiece, but all Gracie cared about was the *beep* that signaled my laptop being turned off—a *beep* Gracie interpreted as a Pavlovian precursor to doggie gratification.

My dog and I had different perceptions about how I chose to spend my days. In between what she perceived as important dog activities (hiking and eating), she had to endure what I considered important human work (writing for a living).

From my point of view, I was being incredibly self-disciplined, maxing out my creativity to write the great American screenplay. But from Gracie's point of view, I was sitting motionless for hours, pawing at tiny plastic squares while staring at a glowing box.

What was she thinking as I performed my silly ritual? Did she wonder if I was staring into that glowing box for the same reason she and her kind occasionally zoned out and stared into space? Did she figure I was warming myself by the glow of the laptop because I was cold? Did she assume some higher power was commanding me to "sit" and "stay" in that chair—like an obedient dog?

From Gracie's perspective, all I did was sit in a chair for hours, wasting a perfectly good sunny day. All I did was stare into a glowing box with my fingers tapping over funny little plastic kiblets that didn't smell appetizing and were not edible. That was definitely not how she'd have spent her time. If things were reversed and she'd been my master, she'd never have let me fritter away long hours doing something as cockamamie as writing. We'd have gone for walks morning, noon, and night; sniffed things; and eaten six times a day. In between all that, we'd have napped.

But I was the boss, so while I wrote, Gracie had to sit and wait. She couldn't understand that what I did earned the money to buy her food and provided the house she slept in and the gas to drive her to the mountains for the walks she loved. But to Gracie's credit, she knew I was her master and allowed me to have my way. Except for an occasional impatient look—or a hint of hunger in her eyes— she always let me do what I had to do.

Just like Gracie, I sit at the feet of my Master, filled with all kinds of yearnings and desires. I'm looking to Him constantly, hoping He will gratify me. I want my screenplay sale now. I want my new car now. "Please God, stop sitting motionless, staring into the heavens, frivolously doing whatever gibberish You are doing in my life. It's time to get up from Your throne and grant my wishes!"

But I don't understand God's ways and thoughts any more than Gracie understands mine. And I don't need to. I just need to keep my eyes on Him. He may not always give me what I want when I want it, but He gives me so much more. He gives me Himself. I can bask in His glow. Just as sunlight is essential for plant growth, Sonlight is essential for my spiritual growth.

If I had to sum up the greatest reward I've received from screenwriting, it's this: I've gotten to know Christ much better. While I've been concerned about my physical and ego needs (selling scripts and earning the praise of my peers), God has been concerned about building my character. He has used my struggles and disappointments to refine my mind and heart.

As the old adage goes, "God works in mysterious ways." And I don't need to understand them all, any more than Gracie did. Like Gracie, I've experienced my Master's love, and I know He will give me what I *really* need, and do what's best for me.

"For my thoughts are not your thoughts, neither are your ways my ways," declares the LORD. "As the heavens are higher than the earth, so are my ways higher than your ways and my thoughts than your thoughts" (Isaiah 55:8-9).

Consider This

Is there something God is doing, or not doing, in your life that seems mysterious to you? What about it is puzzling? What about it is frustrating? Are you able to trust Him in it, or are you struggling? Why?

Illness and Stillness
God Gives Us Quiet Times

Be still, and know that I am God.

PSALM 46:10

When we got Huxley, he seemed especially grateful to be part of our family. He came from a facility where he'd likely have been put to death. I'm sure he didn't know how great his danger was, but I think he was glad to be out of that cage and into our home and big yard.

We'd had Huxley for just a few weeks when he started getting sick. He stopped running and playing. Then he lay down and wouldn't get up. He looked awful, and we could tell that he felt awful too. We hurried him off to the vet, who diagnosed him with a potentially life-threatening illness. The vet gave us medicine and special formula for Huxley. He said if Huxley took his medicine and ate this special, easily digested food, he might live.

We made a comfortable bed for Huxley and checked on him day and night. We all prayed and cried over him. We fed him the food by putting it on our fingertips and placing our fingers in his mouth. There were times when he looked up at us with his sick puppy eyes as if to say he couldn't even try to eat. But we kept on praying and petting him and talking gently to him. We had faith he'd get well.

Eventually, Huxley began looking better, and before long he was back to his old healthy self. He wasn't meant to die as a puppy. He had a special purpose for living. He was our wonderful watchdog and pet for more than 15 years.

We felt that God gave us that time with Huxley to show us how important it was to take time to be quiet and pray. This was a lesson we could use in many parts of our lives. Before Huxley's puppy days were over, I had to learn it all over again.

It was December. We were all very busy with Christmas activities. I came down with a cold, but I didn't take time to rest. How could I? There was too much to do. We even had relatives coming from out of state for the holidays.

We went camping at the beach with about 20 members of our extended family. We had a great time, but I was feeling tired. I was doing a lot of coughing too. By the time we got home and said goodbye to the out of towners, I was in bad shape.

I'd given Huxley the time to be sick, but I didn't want to give time to me. Our three children were very young, and Steve's work was demanding. I had a load of responsibilities I thought only I could handle. Steve's grandma was hospitalized, and his parents were away. *I can't be sidelined now!* I thought.

God thought otherwise. When Steve took his very reluctant wife to the hospital, I was diagnosed with a bad case of pneumonia.

I stayed in the hospital for four days. Friends and family came to see me, but when visiting hours were over, I was terribly lonely. Late on the third night, I was so congested and tired, I thought I might die. I got out of bed, stood by the window, and phoned my mom.

"No, honey, you aren't going to die," Mom comforted me. "You are actually getting better." Then she told me something she had read somewhere. When we have an illness, God may be calling us into stillness. "Remember that while you are praying," she urged. "Good night, honey. I love you."

I lay back down and mulled over those words. *God calls us into stillness.* Here I'd been complaining about my quiet room. I'd been chafing at my hospital stay. But all the while, God was giving me a chance for stillness. Obviously, I had forgotten stillness was something that still existed.

Now I thanked my heavenly Father for giving me this time of stillness. Yet, I asked that He heal me soon, so I could return to my family. Earlier, I had thought my life was over. Now I could see new purpose in it. That night, I slept like a baby. I woke up feeling much, much better. I was sent home the following day.

Just like Huxley, it wasn't my time to die. It was simply a time to be still. Lying there, quiet and alone, gave me time to pray. And it gave me time to listen for my Father's voice. When my nurse came in, I told her what I'd learned through all of this. She thanked me with tears in her eyes. She said she hadn't been scheduled to be in my room, but God must have planned it for her.

Through Huxley's illness, and through mine, we all grew in our prayer life and faith. And we learned to be grateful for the times we can come apart with Him. My goal is to live for God every day, and to thank Him for times of stillness.

*Be still before the L*ord *and wait patiently for him (Psalm 37:7).*

Consider This

Is there a time in your life when God called you into stillness? What did you learn? How has it helped you grow? Do you set time aside on a regular basis to be still before the Lord?

Paw in Glove

Join Forces for God

*When he took time to help the man up
the mountain, lo, he scaled it himself.*

PROVERB

Not every dog is cut out for farming, but Huxley was. He loved going out to work in the fields with Steve. When Steve was irrigating a field, he and Huxley would walk it together. Narrow strips of dry land about two feet high, three feet wide, and as much as a thousand feet long stretched like ribbons between the expanses of water. Steve and Huxley would trudge across these long skinny islands, searching for gophers.

Gophers are a serious problem for farmers. They dig through these islands of dry land, messing up irrigation by congesting the water flow. It's amazing to see the damage a community of gophers can do to a field that farmers have cared for and worked on so long. Steve and Huxley joined their talents together to get rid of these pests. Steve used his two hands and a shovel. Huxley used his nose.

Huxley would walk ahead of Steve, his nose close to the ground, checking for a gopher scent. If there weren't any gophers near, he'd move on. But if he smelled one, he'd lift his head and look at Steve as if to say, "Here he is. Go get 'im!"

Steve was grateful for Huxley's skilled nose and built-in gift of smelling the gophers, which told Steve where to dig to catch them. Huxley loved helping his master.

It's wonderful when a man and his wife can too.

Steve and I have been married for 33 years. We've enjoyed doing things together. We've enjoyed being partners and combining our varied talents. This has served us well, especially in the bumpy times Steve and I call P.O.T.A. (part of the adventure).

The wheel mishap was a P.O.T.A. moment. It was afternoon. Steve was driving a giant tractor down the road. Suddenly, he sensed something was wrong. Then, to his horror, he saw one of his huge tractor wheels roll in front of him. Somehow, it had come loose. I walked outside just in time to watch the runaway wheel head into our neighbor's front yard. The wheel kept going, aiming for the garage. But it hit their fence first, flattened it, and landed in their backyard. Luckily their dog, who had access to the yard, wasn't near.

John had been driving a truck farther down the road, and he had seen the whole thing. He and Steve knew exactly how to handle the wheel and tractor. Handling the neighbor was another matter. Steve had always trusted me more than himself when it came to communication, so he asked me to call and explain what had happened.

Our neighbor wasn't home at the time, but I knew how to reach him. I dialed the number. When he answered, I said, "Hi, this is Connie. I just called to tell you we will keep your dog at our house until you return."

"Oh, you don't need to do that," he said. "We have a fence."

I took a deep breath. "Well, actually, you don't."

"Sure we do," he insisted, sounding more nervous now.

"Not anymore." I explained how our tractor wheel had knocked it down. He was understanding about the mishap, and we got it all worked out, thanks to Steve and me combining our talents to do it.

Steve also likes to join his gifts with others in our local church body. He plays his trumpet and sings on the praise team. And though he's quiet, he tries to encourage newcomers and make them feel welcome. That's how he and Al started getting to know each other.

Al hadn't been to church in several years when he came to visit ours. Steve noticed the stranger and asked him his name. He greeted Al by name the next week. Al was impressed. He was drawn to Steve. As their friendship grew, Steve ministered to Al in any way he could.

Finally, Al decided he would like to be baptized. Steve realized our pastor's teaching gifts were needed now. The pastor helped Al understand what it meant to follow Jesus. Al went through classes. On a beautiful Sunday afternoon, Steve and our pastor stood with Al in a church member's swimming pool and baptized him together.

Steve did his part. Our pastor did his. And God was glorified. That's how He intends things to work in the church, Christ's body. He makes us different so we'll join together to fulfill His purposes. And when we do, we're blessed—just like Steve and Huxley were.

Just as each of us has one body with many members, and these members do not all have the same function, so in Christ we who are many form one body, and each member belongs to all the others. We have different gifts, according to the grace given us. If a man's gift is prophesying, let him use it in proportion to his faith. If it is serving, let him

serve; if it is teaching, let him teach; if it is encouraging, let him encourage; if it is contributing to the needs of others, let him give generously; if it is leadership, let him govern diligently; if it is showing mercy, let him do it cheerfully (Romans 12:4-8).

Consider This

What are your human gifts and talents? What are your spiritual ones? Who might you team with to use them for God's glory?

Wait!

God's Timing Is Perfect

Set not your Loaf in,
till the Oven's hot.

THOMAS FULLER

When I got my dogs, I hired a trainer to teach me to teach them. One command he stressed was "wait." He urged me to use the "wait" command to halt them behind boundaries. He said they must not cross the line without permission, whether it was the threshold of a room or the curb between sidewalk and street. Some day, this might save their lives.

I soon saw what he meant.

I started walking Morgan and Biscuit around my neighborhood. My eager-beaver canines did not always stop at corners. Now and then, they would leap off the curb before I'd checked for traffic. Though they were on leash, they had just enough rope to put themselves at risk. The "wait" command might have done the trick, but I chose to go a step further. I told them to "sit" when we came to a corner. After glancing both ways, I'd say "let's go" and we'd cross the street together.

Of course, the dogs didn't realize their danger. They had no idea why it was I made them wait. But they'd learned to trust and obey me, so they did what I asked.

Sometimes we must trust and obey our Master's "wait" when we don't understand…as dear friends of mine did.

These friends, Bob and Julie, met at a Christian singles group. They started dating. In time, their relationship deepened. It seemed their temperaments and gifts were well suited to each other. They were deeply in love. They began to talk of marriage.

But a barrier loomed. Julie's family was vehemently opposed to the union. They felt they had compelling reasons, and they honestly believed they were acting in Julie's best interests.

Bob and Julie agonized over the matter. They counseled with godly friends who knew them well. They searched their hearts and Scripture. They concluded God was telling them to sit at the corner.

Hard as it was, Bob and Julie obeyed. They worked on their personal growth and their walk with the Lord. They started to realize what might have happened if they'd stepped off the curb. They came to believe that because of their personalities and family backgrounds, they both might have found it hard to form their own strong family unit. This might have hurt or even threatened their marriage, had they gone ahead when they wanted to. Now they were maturing…but Julie's family hadn't changed their minds.

Time passed. Bob and Julie stayed friends. They stayed single. They still cared deeply for each other, but it seemed they would never cross the street into marriage. Julie felt the clock ticking. She longed for a husband. She looked around. She dated a little, but it wasn't right. Then she sensed God saying, "You've been seeking, but you haven't asked Me." She submitted her desires to the Lord. More time passed.

And then, a woman Bob knew began taking a romantic interest in him. When she learned of it, Julie felt a huge pang of loss. And she found herself wondering if there might yet be a chance for her and Bob to be together.

Once again, Julie counseled with godly friends. Once again, she sought the Lord, fasting, praying, and searching the Scriptures. She was committed to doing God's will, not her own. She sensed confirmation from many sources that her desires in the matter were God's also. At last, she felt a release deep within. A weight lifted. She sensed an assurance from the Lord that He would bless her marriage to Bob and take care of her family's hearts.

One final precaution seemed in order. A close mutual friend of the pair spoke with Bob alone—to see if he had reservations. Bob didn't. Instead, he broke down and wept with joy. More than ten years after they'd first met, God was tugging at Bob's and Julie's hearts, and clearly, unmistakably saying, "Let's go!"

Julie's family wasn't thrilled at the turn of events. Still, they didn't forbid the union. Plans went forward. As the wedding drew nearer, Julie's family met with the couple. The big day arrived, and Bob and Julie became husband and wife. It seemed a miracle.

A still greater miracle occurred in the months that followed. God kept His promise to soften Julie's family's hearts. Bob's love and respect won them over. They told Julie they were glad she'd married Bob and said he was an asset to the family.

The Old Testament is filled with examples of God telling His people to wait. Among the most famous is the story of a shepherd boy named David. God chose him to succeed Saul as king over Israel. The prophet Samuel anointed him. But in the years that followed, Saul persecuted David and even tried to kill him. Yet David refused to lift a hand against his oppressor. He knew God had made Saul king, and God must remove him. David waited on the Lord. In time, Saul was defeated in battle and died. God raised up the shepherd boy who had waited to be not only king, but the man through whose lineage the Messiah would be born.

I love Morgan and Biscuit and want to keep them from harm's way. My Master loves me infinitely more. I can trust His "wait," knowing it is for my good, and His timing is perfect.

*Wait for the L*ORD*; be strong and take heart and wait for the L*ORD *(Psalm 27:14).*

Consider This

Is there an area of your life where you think God is saying "wait"? Are you confused, or can you see a purpose in it? What might God want you to work on while you're waiting?

How Long Is Your Lead?
Give Grace, As God Does

It is the spirit and not the form of
law that keeps justice alive.

Earl Warren

Morgan was always a jumper and climber. It could be a challenge to contain him. But there were places I didn't want this dog to go. In particular, I didn't want him sneaking down my back stairs. At the bottom of those steps were things that could get him in trouble. But the stairs descended from the kitchen/den part of my home. This was where I liked to leave the dogs when I went out. Gating Morgan was useless. He just jumped the barrier. So when I left him unattended, I leashed him instead.

The leash was intended as a boundary to keep my dog within the law. I didn't want it to be overly restrictive. So I slipped its looped end under the leg of a kitchen bar stool (probably not a safe thing to do, in retrospect). This way he would have enough lead to stroll around a bit and even reach his water dish if he got thirsty.

Alas, I often returned to find Morgan had modified the arrangement, and not for his benefit. He'd managed to wind his leash around the stool's legs. That gave him almost no rope at all. He'd hog-tied himself to the bar stool and lay trapped beside it. I, his master, never meant to confine him that much.

Reflecting on Morgan's predicament made me realize the need to apply our Master's rules in the way that He intends. Otherwise, the spirit of the law may be defeated. I saw a small example of this at summer camp when I was 13.

The camp was a last-minute choice, inspired by some second cousins I'd just met. All of us were Jewish, but I was Reformed. They were Orthodox. So was the camp. Nearly everyone there was steeped in fine points of Jewish religious law that I had never observed and knew little about.

One night my bunkmates decided to tease me. The Sabbath had started. They asked me to turn on a light. When I did, they pounced. I had broken the Sabbath. Flipping the light switch was work.

The fourth commandment says, "Remember the Sabbath day by keeping it holy. Six days you shall labor and do all your work, but the seventh day is a Sabbath to the LORD your God. On it you shall not do any work" (Exodus 20:8-10).

Just what it means to do work on the Sabbath has been further interpreted through the centuries. Specialists in Jewish law wrote rules to define it. Whatever one thinks of this practice, whether or not one agrees with all the law's fine points, this much is clear. These kids did what neither God nor the law's interpreters intended. The Sabbath rules were meant to set one day a week apart as a day of rest and fellowship with God…not to trip and tease an uninformed teenager.

At that very same camp, in that very same summer, I saw a rule applied in a way that gave grace, and upheld its spirit. It, too, had to do with the Sabbath.

My first Saturday at camp found me bent double in agony. A pain in my right side had kept me up all night. I dragged myself to religious services, trying to ignore the voice in my head that warned I might have appendicitis.

The pain got worse. I went to the infirmary. They put me in a bed and watched me for a couple of hours. My pain kept growing.

I was running a fever now. I needed a higher level of medical attention, but the closest hospital was some distance away.

Driving a car was also defined as doing work on the Sabbath, but it was allowed in medical emergencies. The camp's medical personnel whisked me off for treatment. Before day's end, surgeons had removed my leaking appendix. I got well and lived to write the tale.

Leashes and rules are for our good, but they can be twisted for harm. That's why we must know and uphold the *spirit* of the law. I've done that with Morgan. I don't tie him to a bar stool anymore. I became concerned that one day he'd pull it over on himself. And besides, I found a better way to contain him. When I'm going out, I put him in my office and close the door. He can't get down my back stairs, and he can move around freely. I have given him grace... which our Master also gives us, and wants us to give each other.

He [Jesus] answered, "Have you never read what David did when he and his companions were hungry and in need? In the days of Abiathar the high priest, he entered the house of God and ate the consecrated bread, which is lawful only for priests to eat. And he also gave some to his companions." Then he said to them, "The Sabbath was made for man, not man for the Sabbath" (Mark 2:25-27).

Consider This

Is there an area of your life where you might be winding a leash too tightly, either for yourself or others? What do you think is the spirit of the leash? Is it being upheld? If not, how could you correct this?

How to Handle an Owie
Our Pain Can Serve God's Purpose

No pain, no balm; no thorns, no throne;
no gall, no glory; no cross, no crown.

WILLIAM PENN

Morgan is a very pain-sensitive dog. Any twinge makes him shriek like a banshee. His high-pitched squeal sends me flying half out of my skin. I've wondered if sometimes he yelps in mere anticipation of hurt. Whatever the case, his owies are usually short-lived.

But on this day, things just got worse. The trouble began after breakfast. I was at my computer, and Morgan was under my desk. Suddenly, he yelped, and not just once. I checked him out. He seemed sensitive on one of his front shoulders. I thought perhaps his leg was tweaked and hoped the problem was minor. But as the day progressed, I could see he was not his normal, happy, active self.

That afternoon, I was working out on some home exercise equipment. The dogs were with me, watching, as they often do. Morgan jumped from a couch in the room to the floor, gave a piercing shriek, and curled motionless. He didn't want to budge, for fear he'd trigger his hurt again.

My little guy was engaging in classic pain avoidance. But I, his master, knew his tactic wouldn't work for long. It wouldn't address the cause of the problem, or let him get on with his life. So I did what he needed…I bundled him off to the vet. Luckily, the problem was minor, and with mild treatment, his symptoms speedily subsided.

What hasn't subsided is my image of Morgan, lying frozen, trying not to hurt. I am not that different than my dog in my approach to pain. I, too, try desperately to avoid it. My method is to curl motionless in procrastination, but my Master has shown me that this doesn't work and will often create a worse hurt. Never was this more true than when my dad was dying.

As an only child and an only daughter, I was very close to Dad. Growing up, I all but worshipped him. He had sterling ethics and a brilliant mind. I thought he had never met a problem he couldn't solve. But he also had an iron will. It seemed that whenever I bucked him, he won. Though I loved him deeply, I also felt overpowered by him and overdependent on him, and resented both.

Then, when I was 29, Dad was diagnosed with prostate cancer that had spread to his bones. From the start, he said he feared he was a "gone goose." Mom wouldn't accept that and clung to hope. Despite his gloom, Dad tried to fight back, turning inward and focusing all his efforts on doing what he did best…solving a problem.

By now, I was living and working in L.A., 90 minutes from my parents. I had a housemate, a church, and a relationship with God. I tried to bring these resources to bear in dealing with the situation. At first, I visited. But Dad's illness was bringing my own jumbled feelings about our relationship forward. When my emotional pain got worse, I did what Morgan did. I curled motionless and froze.

For me, freezing meant I stayed in L.A. and didn't go see my dad for more than two months in the winter of that year. I also started battling an old bugaboo, compulsive eating. At some point,

I started seeing a counselor. My father was consuming my thoughts, but I still wasn't visiting him. Perhaps I was trying to duck the pain of a face-to-face look at what he was going through. Other aspects of life also felt overwhelming. But it was a bad choice.

The pattern was finally broken in March when Dad spent a couple of weeks in the hospital at UCLA. I lived minutes away. I couldn't hide anymore. I spent time with both him and Mom.

My parents went home. More time passed. Did I see them? How much? I don't recall. It's a blur to me now. But I still remember, if vaguely, one evening in early May. I was in my car, and I felt an impulse, a nudge, to head for my parents' house. I acted on it. I spent the weekend, returning on a Sunday night. Early Monday morning, convinced he was dying anyway, unwilling to be a burden, and tired of the intense physical suffering he was enduring, my father took his life. Too late, I wished I had faced the pain and taken more time to be with him while I could.

My pain avoidance hadn't worked. It had led to worse hurt…the pain of regret and guilt. But my merciful Master had given me one last weekend with Dad nonetheless. And He used my sin and my pain to teach me a difficult lesson. I learned that in life, you don't always get a rewrite.

Humanly, we want to duck our pain. Even Jesus felt this way. But He chose to suffer so that we might be saved. One man died for many, and God's purpose was fulfilled. And after He'd suffered, Jesus knew the joy of having glorified His Father.

Often pain seems pointless, but God may use it in ways we'd never dream. If we let God use our pain for His purpose, we will glorify Him too.

Now if we are children, then we are heirs—heirs of God and co-heirs with Christ, if indeed we share

in his sufferings in order that we may also share in his glory (Romans 8:17).

Consider This

Do you have a hurt in your life right now that makes you want to curl up motionless? What might happen if you did this? If you didn't? Does God feel near or far in your pain? Can you confide in a fellow believer who might help you bear your burden?

Little Doggie
Lesser Things Prepare Us for Greater

*The right performance of this hour's
duties will be the best preparation for
the hours or ages that follow it.*

RALPH WALDO EMERSON

Getting Gracie was a big step for me. It was the first time in my adult life that I was entrusted with the welfare of a living thing beyond the scope of low-risk tropical fish or houseplants. If I withheld food, water, or medical care, Gracie would die. But for more than ten years, I was a good master. I kept her alive, happy, and loved.

It's no secret to my friends and family that Gracie helped me ease into the role of becoming a father. I had been one of those confirmed bachelor types who didn't spend much time thinking about having my own family. No matter what my chronological age was, I always thought of myself as a kid. Everyone else was the adult.

But Gracie helped me grow up. Cleaning up after Gracie in the yard prepared me for changing Skye's diapers. Bathing a reluctant Gracie was good training for bathing a squirming, uncooperative little boy. And disciplining my dog with a rolled-up newspaper gave me confidence I could mete out a spanking or two to a way-ward toddler.

God, in His wisdom, gave me Gracie before He gave me Skye. Like elementary school prepares you for high school, which pre-pares you for college—caring for and loving a dog better prepared me to be my son's dad.

I am seeing a similar godly process take place with Skye. He just turned four, and for the past couple of years, his closest pal (besides his parents) has been a stuffed dog named Little Doggie. He sleeps with this little tan plush toy every night. He has animated talks with Little Doggie. He sits his stuffed dog up on toy cars, trucks, and trains. He puts Little Doggie on his tricycle handlebars and rides him around the living room. At mealtimes, Skye props up Little Doggie on the dining table as a fourth member of our family. When Skye was younger, he often refused to eat until his best friend was fed first with a spoonful of cereal or a sip of milk. Little Doggie is as real to Skye as Gracie was to me.

Skye was three years old when Gracie died. He never knew her the way I did—as a playful, frisky pup. But he still remembers her, and once in a while, he asks if he can have a real dog of his own someday. It warms my heart, because I know he'll make a great dog person. As Skye gives his stuffed dog food and drink—as he trains, plays with, cuddles, pets, and most of all, loves Little Doggie—so, I am confident, he will one day care for a real dog.

Watching Skye and Little Doggie gives me a glimpse into God's great and timeless wisdom. It is His way to first entrust us with less—and if we are faithful in that, then He is happy to give us more.

In the parable of the talents, a master entrusted small sums of money to three of his servants. Two of the servants were wise and doubled their funds. Their master was well pleased with these fel-lows and rewarded them with a greater trust. However, the third servant buried his money in the ground and did nothing with it. Because he was unfaithful in less, he not only wasn't entrusted with more, he was punished and lost even the little he had.

In the same manner, if I saw that Skye was not wise in the welfare of Little Doggie—if he pulled off his stuffed tail, lit him on fire, or tried to flush him down the toilet—I'd think twice about giving him a real dog.

Likewise, if our all-knowing heavenly Master sees that we are not wise and faithful in dealing with the lesser things He sends our way—things that may appear menial and beneath us—He may think twice about allowing us to move on to the greater things our hearts desire.

In the film *The Karate Kid*, the hero eagerly desires to be trained to fight by a karate master, but all the master has the kid do is wax cars. Though the kid complains, he eventually does his lowly job with excellence. Later, he discovers the menial and repetitious "wax on, wax off" motions were preparing him to execute secret karate moves with excellence—to give him victory over his more powerful opponent.

As Gracie prepared me for a son, as Little Doggie prepares Skye for a real dog, God is using your lesser things to prepare you for more. And who knows what amazing things God may have in store for those who are faithful to Him?

His master replied, "Well done, good and faithful servant! You have been faithful with a few things; I will put you in charge of many things. Come and share your master's happiness!" (Matthew 25:21).

Consider This

Is there an area of your life where you feel you have something lesser and desire something greater? How might God be using this lesser thing to prepare you? How can you be faithful and wise in less, so God can entrust you with more?

Alpha and Omega
We Are Useful to God, Whatever Our Age

A new broom sweeps clean, but
an old one knows the corners.

When McPherson came to our family, Steve and I were just 21 years old. I guess you could say that we were all puppies together. We lived in a little farmhouse just in front of the home Steve grew up in. McPherson was a shepherd mix and full of energy. He would race through the house, often knocking things over, like the mug that held Steve's morning coffee. He liked to chew on Steve's socks and my favorite athletic shoes. But what McPherson loved best was just being with us. He'd curl up next to us while we read or watched TV. When he got a little older, he'd go off to work with Steve and chase gophers. He was a faithful pup, and grew more faithful as time went on.

McPherson moved with us from the small farmhouse to the big old farmhouse built by Steve's grandpa. He was four when our oldest child, Christy, was born. As she grew to be a toddler,

McPherson was Christy's companion and protector, running with her, fetching balls, and watching out for her.

By the time our middle child, John, was a toddler, McPherson was eight. He couldn't run as fast as before, but his love was even stronger. He snuggled with the children and with us, and tried to keep up with them as best he could.

McPherson was 11 when Karen, our youngest, reached toddler age. He didn't chase balls anymore. He watched while the kids played, but he still did his best to protect them. If a visitor drove into the yard while they were outside, he kept a careful eye on the stranger. Even at the end, when his body was failing, McPherson never gave up his place in the family, and his love for us never wavered. He always did what he could.

My mother's love has never wavered, either. Like McPherson, she has always done what she could. All her life, her ministry has been to serve people.

When I was little, I watched my mom work in the church kitchen. She taught me how to prepare lovely dishes of food and how to serve them. She also loved cooking for family, friends, or anyone else who just needed a good meal.

Along with the wonderful meals she made, Mom served up encouragement. She had a kind word for everyone. Often, kids who came to the house would ask her for advice. She always ended the conversation by promising to pray for them...and she did.

When I reached my teen years and joined the Youth for Christ club at my high school, Mom took charge of finding people to make sandwiches for our meetings. Other parents were often too busy, so they'd give her money for ingredients and she'd put the food together herself. On Tuesday mornings, every flat area in our kitchen, dining room, and living room was covered with bread to make sandwiches for the 450 students who came to our club. Mom didn't attend the meetings herself, but as she was preparing our food, she'd pray for the Youth for Christ director and all the students who would be there that day.

Dad died when I was 21. Mom now felt she needed to do some work outside the home. She cooked meals for the local Kiwanis Club and Christian Businessmen's Club. She hired me to help her. We liked working together and chatting with the members. There were always people coming to Mom for encouragement or advice. She would talk with them and promise to pray, just as she had with my childhood friends. They always left with a smile.

Mom is still bringing smiles to people's lips and encouraging them some 30 years later. She has just moved into a wonderful retirement home. She thought it would be a good idea, and that she could have a ministry there. Almost daily she goes to a tea party they have for the residents. She's not involved in preparing the food, but she listens to others, as she always has, and shares what the Lord has done for her, and what He can do for them.

Both Mom and McPherson demonstrate that God can use us whatever our age. I have found that to be true in my own life as well. For years, Steve and I have served on our church's kitchen committee, and also on the music and drama teams.

When our children were in elementary school, I helped start their school's Moms in Touch ministry. We got together once a week for an hour to pray. We'd lift up the school, students, staff, and any concerns that came to our attention. Now and then we brought the staff special treats to show our appreciation. Years later, when I became a teacher myself, I was prayed for by the Moms in Touch group at the school where I taught.

I don't have children in school anymore, and I no longer teach full-time anywhere, but I still have a ministry of prayer. I'm on my church's prayer chain. I am also involved with a group of professionals in the entertainment industry who meet to worship and pray together. Whatever my age, no matter where I am or how I feel, I know I can always pray, and this is something God wants me to do.

"There is a time for everything, and a season for every activity under heaven" (Ecclesiastes 3:1). As we age, we may not be able to do all the things we could in our youth. But we may have added wisdom and experience to offer. And God can still use us mightily, if our hearts are willing and open to His leading. If our love is strong, like McPherson's and Mom's, and we're willing to serve, we will always have a purpose in the family of God.

I will pour out my Spirit on all people. Your sons and daughters will prophesy, your old men will dream dreams, your young men will see visions (Joel 2:28).

Consider This

What are some ways you feel that God is using you right now? How are they different from how He has used you in the past? How are they similar or related?

If you feel your life lacks purpose, are you willing to seek God's leading and follow it?

Meet the Authors

M.R. Wells has written extensively for children's animated television and video programming, including several Disney shows, the animated PBS series *Adventures from the Book of Virtues,* and the live action video series *Bibleman.* She has also been developing a fantasy fiction trilogy. She lives in California with her two dogs, Morgan and Biscuit, and three cats.

Kris Young has worked as a screenwriter for more than 20 years and currently teaches screenwriting at the L.A. Film Studies Center and UCLA. He lives in the foothills of Southern California with his wife, Celine, and son, Skye. His dog, Gracie, passed away during the writing of this book.

Connie Fleishauer is a teacher as well as a writer, producer, director, and actor with Whistle Wickert Productions. She is the wife of a California farmer and the mother of three grown children. She is friend and master to her beloved Welsh corgi, Stuart.